# *My Father's Gospel*

## DR. HAROLD CARTER JR.

*My Father's Gospel: Reminiscences of a Son*
by Harold Carter Jr.

© Copyright 2016

SAINT PAUL PRESS, DALLAS, TEXAS

First Printing, 2016

All rights reserved. No part of this publication may be reproduced, stored in a retrieval system, or transmitted in any form or by any means, electronic, mechanical, photocopying, recording, or otherwise, without the prior permission of the copyright owner, except for brief quotations included in a review of the book.

Cover layout by Harold A. Carter Jr.
Cover design by Bellart Graphics
Cover (front) portrait by Carlton D. O'Neal
Cover (back, top) photo by Thomas ("Hollywood") Henderson
Cover (back, bottom) photo by Donald E. Lee
    (taken at the Dead Sea, Jordan/West Bank)

---

ISBN-10: 1533603464
ISBN-13: 978-1533603463

Printed in the U.S.A.

To my sister
*Weptanomah Carter Davis*
our father's devoted caregiver.

 # Contents

Acknowledgments ....................................................... 9
Foreword ................................................................... 11
Introduction ............................................................. 17

1. The Gospel of Detroit ........................................ 21
2. The Gospel of Biscuits ...................................... 33
3. The Gospel of "It's Yours" ................................ 45
4. The Gospel of Self-Inspiration ......................... 55
5. The Gospel of Adventure
   and a Pioneering Spirit ..................................... 73
6. The Gospel of Dr. Quick-Prayer ...................... 89
7. The Gospel of the Enigmatic Preacher .......... 101
8. The Gospel of Succession .............................. 117

Notes ..................................................................... 135
Bibliography .......................................................... 137
About the Author ................................................. 139

#  *Acknowledgments*

To my wonderful and loving wife with a grateful heart for her inspiration and input in bringing this work to completion.

To my "successive" sons, Daniel (Rev.) and Timothy.

To my New Shiloh Church family for being the people who embraced my father for forty-eight years.

To my dedicated executive secretary, Mrs. Jamelia Ward, who, once again, worked through and processed more than a half dozen drafts and formatted the same for publication.

To God be the Glory!

# Foreword

There was a time many years ago when my brother, the author of the book, and I were traveling with our parents, the tour leaders of a group, making a pilgrimage to the Holy Land. As we were boarding the boat to cross the Sea of Galilee, our dad started saying he was going to walk on the water (like Peter after Jesus bid him come). By the time we got on the boat, members of our pilgrimage were excited to see if Dr. Carter was going to get out and walk on the water. This was one of the early sojourns that we were blessed to take. I was young and kind of scared. Could he really do it? What if it did not work? Our dad had a playful side; really, he was an agitator. It would take a few more years before I learned that, if I paid close attention to my mother, I could tell what was going on with my father. However, my brother was all in for Daddy's walking on water excursion. Whether he thought our father could do it or not, I remember him sitting on the boat with that sly smile and chuckle that is unique to him. In my mind, he seemed to say, *Do it, Daddy, do it.*

I am thrilled that my brother took the time to write this book. He gives a glimpse into the time we spent together as sister and brother in our parents' home. It is, also, his telling of their relationship in shared pastoral ministry. More important, this book speaks of a relationship of a father and son who did not place limits on each other. Their ability to share in each other's happiness and disappointments was seamless. My beloved mother and I were aware of this. Daddy was happy for Mann, as we called him, and Mann was happy for Daddy. As a result, my mother and I were happy about their happiness. For the record, based on the situation, there are numerous adjectives that I could use in the preceding sentence. The sentence would still hold true because they were highly in sync and esteemed the other better than each one esteemed himself.

I believe this was key to our dad's remarkable stamina and longevity after his cancer diagnosis. My brother never saw a patient when he looked at our dad. Along with prayer and the hand of God, this gave life to our dad and empowered him to live significantly past his medical prognosis. My intention was not to become the Martha to what they had between them, though it seemed to me that appointments should be kept and medicine should be taken at the prescribed times, mindful that his loving wife and our dear mother had passed in 2006. Nevertheless, I would be in denial if I did not acknowledge the charge our dad felt when Mann entered the room. Never was this more potent than during the last months of our dad's time on earth. One pastor walked in blessing and saying, "Hey,

Doc"; the other pastor sat up blessing and saying, "Doctor, it's good to see you." It was miraculous to behold and a thousand times more fast acting than the doctor's medicine. As the Bible records it, the father-son relationship is highly significant, much more so than the mother-daughter relationship. This certainly gives the book a point of connection to a biblical relationship witnessed in many incarnations in the Bible. Beyond the father-son connection, this is also a book about familial love.

Everyone in our family of four would agree that Daddy was the embodiment of expressed love in our home. Maybe it was his Southern upbringing that informed his sense that he should always have something to share with others as the author writes in chapter three. It could be his mother's admonition to him and his siblings, that she was "not fattening frogs for snakes," that instilled an expectation that he must be productive and effective. Perhaps, it was his Christmas Eve birthday that made him a jolly and happy fellow. Whatever the contributing factors, our father loved life and did view it as the author writes with a "buoyant quality." Naturally this made for exciting times at Christmas. It would be years before I realized that all families did not open gifts the same way we did. Since our dad was born on Christmas Eve, we always felt that we should give him extra gifts. Regardless, it was hard to outdo him in the sport of gift-giving. As my brother and I got older and started earning money, we tried to come up with standout gifts. Before long, my father coined the term "handclap gift." And when an opened gift was deemed worthy someone would say "that's a handclap gift" and we would clap. I don't remember the gift that precipitated my brother declaring, "That's a standing ovation gift," but when he did everyone fell out laughing and we stood up and clapped.

Over the years, extended family members and friends who shared Christmas with us did not take long to catch on to our family's fun. Naturally, the person who received the most standing ovations for his gift selections was our father. My brother received his fair share as well as our mother. Uncle Nat, our father's beloved brother, Dr. Nathan Carter, was also saluted with his share of standing ovations for his gift selections. No matter the ovations, hand claps, or a "that's nice" (which basically was a C-), at the end of the day, our father always had a stack of gifts left to open. That is because the real thrill for him was to give and make his family happy. For me, to go shopping with Daddy meant that I could not study anything too long or hard lest he think I wanted it and he would buy it. I would say, "I like to study things, Daddy. I enjoy looking at things. It doesn't mean I want it." I'm certain these kinds of interactions with my dad held true for my mother, brother, and probably others as well.

This is an aspect of our father that my brother details in a way that ties together our dad's fundamental belief about his desire to serve and bless others. The prized beauty of his life is that he was so happy doing what he did. Last November (2015), during the week of Thanksgiving, I made a daily grateful post on Instagram. The day I posted a picture of our parents, taken at my wedding, it quickly became my most popular post. One comment in particular made me happy and teary. It read, "They were awesome. I miss them too. They were such a blessing and

I loved your father's smile."

I salute my brother for thinking enough of our father and their relationship to document it for posterity. If you were blessed to know Dr. Harold Carter, this book will be a delightful journey through fond memories. If you never had the pleasure of meeting him, this book will provide a moving and intimate view of a unique father-son pastoral relationship. For me, however, as the only daughter of Dr. Carter and the only sister of the author, this book is a treasure that captures precious elements of our family.

We used to sing a song, "I'm so glad Jesus lifted me." There is a line in that song, "Satan had me bound, Jesus lifted me." Harold Carter, until he shook off his earthly robe, lived every day determined to shake off anything that bound him. He enjoyed life as a man set free, set free to live and set free to love.

Weptanomah B. Carter Davis

# *Introduction*

Having been called to serve the congregation of the New Shiloh Baptist Church, Baltimore, MD, in October, 1996, in what I've termed over the years as a mutual pastoral ministry with my father, both of us were frequently asked how it came to be. How was it working out? And how were we able to work with each other so well? God truly blessed us to pastor together for seventeen years without a single cross word or conflict. He said to me, during the time that I was praying about and considering the call to be with him at New Shiloh, "If you feel so led to come, I don't see anything but blessings all around." He could not have spoken truer words. On or around my tenth year at New Shiloh, I began to consider doing a Focus Group about biblical succession at United Theological Seminary, Dayton, OH, where I'd been co-mentoring D. Min.

students on Prophetic Preaching with Bishop Rudolph McKissick, Jr., who, during the same period as I had, joined his father in pastoral ministry.

Across the country and across denominational lines and including both African-American and white congregations, the trend was apparently shifting where Pulpit Committees or Search Committees were becoming less prevalent when churches were soon to become vacant and churches were maturing to give their pastors the authority to put in place his or her successor, or at the very least, make a Spirit-led recommendation. I had also done a preliminary outline for a book about biblical succession during that same time.

Actually, this work was supposed to be the result of that outline, but it wasn't long before my thoughts and writings flowed toward more about the telling of my father's spiritual journey and eventually the telling of how I came to be with him in pastoral ministry. The clincher for me in doing this work at this time was that when I'd humbly and prayerfully accepted the church's call to pastor with my father, succeeding him wasn't even on my mind. I came to be *with* him. God knows I would still love for him to be here now. However, it's clear that he saw the bigger picture and prepared for the same as any leader would.

The likelihood is that at some point, having been able to accomplish this work with the help of God, the focus on a work specifically about biblical and/or spiritual succession will come to fruition. It is still a major concept that I'd like to further explore, even beyond the last chapter of this book.

In the meantime, I'm excited about *My Father's Gospel*. It

gave me the wonderful opportunity to trace his life, as well as relive some of our special father-son moments – moments that I enjoy sharing and that would otherwise be left in the vault of my memory. Those of you who came to know him know that he possessed an endearing persona which drew all of us to him. As he represented God's Kingdom here on earth, preaching the Gospel of Jesus Christ, he may not have known it, but in more ways than one, he had become for us our "good news," the personification of the Gospel. Welcome, anew, to his gospel.

# 1

# The Gospel of Detroit

I began writing this chapter on Friday, March 18, the eve of the weekend that I would be returning to preach for the fourth consecutive year at the historic Hartford Memorial Baptist Church where Dr. Charles G. Adams is the Senior Pastor, and his son, Rev. Charles C. Adams, is the Presiding Pastor. I finished the first draft of the same that Sunday evening, March 20, having preached twice that morning. Detroit and Hartford Memorial are extremely significant to me because, when I first came to preach at the church, my father and I had been invited to come together. That Sunday, March 17, 2013, I was privileged to preach during the 8:00 a.m. service and my father preached during the 11:00 a.m. service. It was the first and only time, during the almost seventeen years that we served together in mutual pastoral ministry at the New Shiloh Baptist Church, Baltimore, Maryland, that we had both preached together *on a Sunday, from the same pulpit outside of New Shiloh.*

*He had been going to Hartford Memorial for about ten years, always the third weekend, leading the church's Annual Prayer Conference on Saturday, then preaching for both services on Sunday. As God would have it, four years ago, I was asked to join with him and since his home going, I've been returning. Needless to say, it is an emotional experience. When we ministered there together, he was not in the best of health, but he rallied himself. He had the utmost respect for his friend, Dr. Adams, and he loved the people of Hartford Memorial. He knew that many of them had roots in the South, mindful that their parents and grandparents, etc. had come to Detroit to better their living conditions during the 50's and 60's by working in the automobile industry. He, therefore, felt a connection with them that he would often talk with me about.*

*I must admit, however, that I really hadn't connected the real significance of my father with the city of Detroit until I was halfway through writing/researching this chapter. I was aware that he had worked at Ford Motor Co., but while working there, his brief time in Detroit would change his life.*

\*\*\*\*

My father, the son of a preacher and pastor, grew up around preachers, having been born December 24, 1936. His father was not only a preacher and pastor but a teacher of preachers at Selma University, where he taught Old Testament for fifty years. Selma University, often referred to as SU, was founded after organized slavery for the purpose of providing Christian education to Black students and for the training of ministers who were called to preach the Gospel. It was, interestingly enough, into such an educational environment that my father began kindergarten at the age of four. Students, he told me, had to go to chapel every day. He could not "play hooky" because his father was on staff and would be sitting on the stage. Boys and men had to wear shirts, ties, and jackets. Girls and women had to wear skirts and dresses. No doubt that such daily attire for the males had tremendous influence on my father inasmuch as he wore a suit, tie, and dress shoes just about every day of his adult life.

It must be understood that my father came of age in the post-slavery, post-emancipation days in the Deep South. Grown men who had not been privileged to receive their basic and foundational learning as children were often put together with young persons my father's age in order for them to catch up. A lot of these men were preachers who desired learning the basics in order to better themselves, especially in English, reading, and history.

My father loved to reminisce about himself during these pre-high school days of learning when he was around the age of ten or eleven. He referred to himself as somewhat mischievous. He would tell the story, hardly able to keep himself from laughing hysterically, of sitting behind an older man tickling his ear with a feather, while the poor man kept slapping his ear as if a fly or mosquito was buzzing around him, nipping at his ear. My father even claimed to have had great aim at shooting spit balls in class.

He had his father's influence at home and often rode with him to various preaching engagements and local conferences. He was around preachers as a part of his schooling. And, of course, he was influenced by the pastor of his family's church, Dr. D. V. Jemison, of Tabernacle Baptist Church, who was also the president of the National Baptist Convention of America, Inc. I say, "family's church," because his father pastored several rural churches, two of which I recall attending during the seventies: one in Clanton, AL, and the other in Centerville, AL, both of which were about thirty miles away from the family's home. As was somewhat the norm in the country, he would preach at the churches on alternating Sundays. Fifth Sundays were usually taken as vacation days, although Sunday School would still take place.

He had a tremendous respect for Dr. Jemison, viewing him as a holy man of God, even as one approaching sainthood. He viewed "Tab" (as members affectionately called it) as having an impact on his life where caring people helped to provide him with "a buoyant quality that saw life as a romance rather than a battlefield; an exciting challenge and experience rather than a destructive encounter with forces destined to destroy you before your life got started!"[1]

He fondly recalled his days and experiences at "Tab" as giving balance between the new and powerful gospel experiences of the surrounding churches in the "Black Belt," where African-Americans sang without instruments. He felt that he was able to feed off the prayers of amazing utterance and power, and soul religion which transformed ordinary church houses into sanctuaries... where everyone had a good time and no one was left out. During those formative days of his youth, he also developed a love for the common meter songs of our religious history. Such an appreciation remained with him until the time God called him home. If he couldn't remember the exact words of such songs as an adult, he had no problem coming up with his own, as members of New Shiloh, the church where he would be called to pastor, fondly know.

Music was a vital part of the Carters' family life. His mother and my grandmother, Mrs. (Dr.) Lillie Bell Carter, was an educator, having graduated from Alabama State College in Montgomery, AL. When she met my grandfather, she was an elementary school principal. She left the school system to sacrificially raise her family, which ultimately consisted of three daughters and two sons, my father being the third child. He describes his mother as having the voice of "a ringing bell," which she used not only for singing praises to God as a soloist in services of worship, but to lovingly discipline him and his siblings when necessary. "Daddy preached the gospel and Momma sang the praises of God. Daddy was the saintly moralist while Momma was the disciplinarian providing counsel and expecting the very best from her daughters and her sons," he once mentioned. It was from his father that he gained a great reverence for prayer and the power of living a disciplined life. It was from his mother that he gained a drive to excel and not be satisfied with mediocrity.

Since Tabernacle Baptist Church was in walking distance from the Carter home had a service every Sunday, my father, along with his brother and sisters, would attend there regularly. He also thought of "Tab," which was founded in 1885, as a place of great love where many of the "strong" families of Selma worshipped, although it admittedly had a reputation as the "high class church" where the people did not say "Amen." To the contrary, my father felt such stereotypes weren't exactly fair.

My father loved to reminisce as to how no one really considered him to follow in his father's footsteps as a preacher. He indicated that he was small in physique, playful, and fond of swimming butt (or buck, as some say) naked and fishing in the creek that ran a short distance behind their home. When he wasn't outdoors playing, he found himself helping his mother in the kitchen. Everyone thought that his brother, eleven months his senior, Nathan (whom the family affectionately called, "Brother"), would become the preacher. Not "Lil' Lippy," as his mother familiarly called him. It wasn't until the eleventh grade that he would transfer to the new high school built next door to where his family lived: The R.B. Hudson High School, which was named after an African-American educator from Selma. It was from R.B. Hudson that he graduated in 1952, only to leave home to attend his mother's *alma mater* Alabama State College (now University) at the ripe old age of fifteen.

It was at the age of seven when my father gave his life to Jesus Christ one Sunday morning at "Tab." He shared with me that not long after his doing so that he had a dream. He recounted that the sky he saw in his dream was very dark, but there was a proportionately brilliant light interspersed. Then, stars formed the words in sharp bold letters: YOU ARE CALLED TO PREACH. He kept that dream to himself for years almost through college. He did not want to preach. He told me on more than one occasion, even as I've heard him tell others, that he had been negatively impacted by gossip about "jackleg preachers" and the stereotypes often associated with them, or that kind of caricature that was in the minds of people. He wanted no part of that kind of (his words) sordid and ignorant affair.

He was actually able to get into Alabama State College because of his mother's influence. He wanted to go to Alcorn College in Lorman, MS, on a band scholarship. He had become quite the saxophonist and would eventually play in a rock 'n' roll band called King Tut & the Houserockers, earning a few college dollars. However, his mother had contacted the dean, who was a former classmate of hers, whose name was Dr. Derrick Hardy. He told her, "Send me your son." So, he went to Alabama State on a full work-study program. He ended up working in the dean's office doing administrative type work—filing papers, running the mimeograph machine, etc. In addition to his courses and work, he auditioned and was accepted into the school band, as well as the college choir. Yes, he played a mean axe, but he also had a beautiful tenor singing voice.

His brother was something of a musical prodigy, and he had been accepted at Hampton Institute (now University), Hampton, VA. At one time, his parents had three children in college: the two sons and the oldest daughter. To make ends meet, and in an effort to lessen the burden on his parents, the summer after his sophomore year, he went to stay with an uncle and his family in order to hopefully find work at the Ford Motor Company in Detroit, MI. The year was 1955 and was transformative in his life.

It was while in Detroit that he began thinking about training to be a lawyer. He dreamed of representing his people and becoming a vital part of the Black Liberation Struggle. Inasmuch as he was coming of age, like countless other African-Americans, he was awakening to segregation and the plight of his people. In fact, my sister, Weptanomah, mentioned a story about our father that I was not mindful of. We were able to have it, subsequently, confirmed.

The previous summer after his freshman year, he worked as a short order cook at Craig Air Force Base located five miles outside of Selma. Only a small group of civilian African-Americans were fortunate enough to be employed on the base and most of the jobs were labor intensive.

My father's older sister, Mrs. Dorothy Carter Jackson, who is presently eighty-two years old and lives in the home of their upbringing located on Lapsley Street, recalled the following: Hal (as his siblings called him) along with a few others would leave out early each morning, walk to Carter's Drugstore (no connection) and catch the nickel bus to the base. Others would actually walk to the base since it was just several miles away, but they had to get up and leave a lot earlier.

This incident occurred before Rosa Parks and the Montgomery Bus Boycott; however it was during the time when Negroes were relegated to sit in the back of the bus. If there were no seats in the back, they had to stand. One day, Hal sat down on that nickel bus and didn't move. The white bus driver told him to move but he refused. Fortunately, they got to the base without anything bad happening. I think he must've walked home later that day.

The next day, he did the same thing. This time, one of the

older men who also worked on the base said to Hal that he should move… that if he didn't he was jeopardizing their jobs and he would be the one responsible for fixing it so that none of them (Negroes) would be able to ride that bus, ever again.

My father then got up, but instead of going to the seats in the rear, he only moved back a few rows. His sister said that, in his mind, he was thinking that he was a first-class citizen. (As providence would have it, when Rosa Parks passed in 2005, my father was called upon to offer the prayer during the service that preceded her lying in state/honor, which took place in the Capital Rotunda, in Washington, D.C. It was truly a tremendous honor for him.)

A year later, he still had such a desire to be involved in the liberation movement, but he also knew and felt as though he was really trying to avoid that "other dream." He stated, "I was still seeking to blot out the dream and destroy the consciousness of (that) still small voice that haunted me," which was echoing in his spirit, "That's all right—you are still called to preach."

Several experiences occurred of significance that summer, including his aunt lovingly and often jokingly teasing him saying, "All that lawyer stuff you're talking about… you know you are going to preach. It's all over you." He wondered if she had seen him reading the Bible, especially the Gospel of John, during his quiet time.

When he went to Ford Motor Company to apply for a job one morning, he was turned down. He'd taken the bus and was trying to cross over to the other side of a six-lane boulevard where the bus let him off. Coming from Selma, such traffic was a new experience for him. Eventually, a sensitive and sympathetic driver stopped in the lane closest to him after recognizing his predicament. Then, a driver in the middle lane stopped. He forgot about the third lane on his side of the boulevard and ran directly into the path of a speeding car which missed him only by inches. When he finally got safely across the other three lanes, with cars coming in the opposite direction, he heard an inner voice saying, "Stop running." That afternoon, determined not to give up, he tried again, but was still turned down. He was about to leave the personnel office when his spirit urged him to tell the man at the counter that he was from Selma, AL, and that he was seeking to better his life by earning money to finish college. He shook the man's hand and was turning to leave. The man said, "Be here on Monday and I will give you a job." Before he could get out the door, the man called him back to the counter. "Young man, I am going to sign you up now." He never forgot how God's divine hand made a way for him that day.

The last day of work at Ford, a Polish man drove him to the bus stop (the boulevard had proven to be too much). "So," said the man, "you are going back home. Whatever your father is doing, you must do, also." My father thought, *Wow. How could he know my father is a preacher?*

His brother had worked in Toledo, OH, that same summer. They arranged it so they would meet and ride back to Selma on the Greyhound bus. Together, they shared their experiences, but the scale tilted to "Brother" prodding him to be open to the call that was on his life, as my father had opened up to his brother regarding his call.

The first Sunday after he arrived back at college in Montgomery for the Fall semester, he went to Dexter Avenue Baptist Church to hear their new pastor, Dr. Martin Luther King, Jr. He was able to speak with Dr. King and told him that he had wanted to be a doctor, then a lawyer, but was wrestling with the call to preach. How transformed he felt when Dr. King told him that he had gone to college wanting to be a doctor, then a lawyer, only to accept his call to preach the Gospel. He felt like an enormous weight had been lifted, and in his own words, he was miraculously born again. "It seemed to me that from that time forward, I began a romance with the power of the mind, the thrill of the Spirit, and the satisfying pursuit of the Word of God. A whole new world had opened up for me."[4]

He called home that same Sunday night. His sister, Marian, answered the phone, and before he could even get a word out he heard her, intuitively, say to his mother upon answering the phone, "It's Hal. He's calling home to tell y'all he's been called to preach." She was never more right in her life.

# 2

# The Gospel of Biscuits

My father graduated from Crozer Theological Seminary, Philadelphia, PA, in 1959, where Dr. King was an alumnus and had recommended him to enroll. That same year, he had been called to the pastorate of the Court Street Baptist Church, Lynchburg, VA, founded during the days of slavery in 1833. The church building was quite large for its day. It seated 1,800 persons and had a "horseshoe" balcony. Due to its size, it served the community for most of the meetings associated with the growing Civil Rights Movement.

Prior to relocating to Lynchburg, my father had been invited to preach at the Second Baptist Church in Philadelphia, PA. It was as a result of that preachment that the First Lady, Mrs. Jacqueline Washington, thought well enough of the young seminary preacher from Selma to have him introduced to her second and youngest daughter, Weptanomah. In its obituary column, the *Baltimore Sun* newspaper (Feb. 28, 2006) wrote regarding that portion of her life, including meeting my father, "I made a quick exit through the back door." Of course, she soon returned.

My father blushingly recalled that there was no way such a pretty young woman from the North would have anything to do with him, a rather naïve young man from the Deep South. Yet, as is so often the case, opposites attract.

"I went to Lynchburg alone, but not for very long," he wrote. "On October 17, 1959, I married Weptanomah Bermuda Washington in a ceremony in her father's church. My own father, Dr. N. M. Carter, married us and the whole occasion was a mighty celebration of two ministerial families coming together as one, from two different poles: the religious world of the north and the religious world of the south." [2]

Weptanomah joined him in Lynchburg and helped him begin the transformation of a mainline, traditional congregation to one of evangelism and civic mindedness. The new bride was a pianist and soon had given new life to the Gospel Chorus, which filtered new life into the worship. Her spirit and charm were infectious and won the hearts of many, in essence winning hearts to the new pastor, as well.

The Court Street Church was rewarding, as well as challenging, though. According to my father, it was the only church he ever cursed in while preaching. Generally speaking, the congregation was warm and loving, but they weren't prone to sanctioning the preacher. Having grown accustomed to hearing a few "Amens" and "Preach, preacher," my father said that one Sunday he simply had enough of their silence. So, in his youthful zealousness, he told them to "go to hell." (Note: for him, and many of that era, using the word "hell" in such a way was synonymous with profanity.) He really felt bad about letting his emotions get the best of him that day and vowed never to let that happen again.

While in Lynchburg, my father became more involved in the Civil Rights Movement, participating in marches and speaking at rallies. He was also able to teach Old Testament at Virginia Seminary and College like his father did at SU. It was there where he formed lasting friendships. One such friend was Dr. A. C. D. Vaughn, whom he taught but soon befriended, forming a brotherhood that remained until the day my father died, if not beyond. See, it wasn't long before the newlyweds had their first child in 1960, a beautiful curly-haired baby girl who was given her mother's name, Weptanomah. Then, they had a darling son (me) who was given his father's name, Harold. It was Dr. Vaughn who was given the honor of being our godfather—a relationship that remains intact even at the time of this writing. Another such friend, a student at Virginia Seminary and College (now, Virginia University of Lynchburg), was Rev. Lawrence Carter (now, Dr.). Dr. Carter would serve as an intern, under my father, at the Court Street Baptist Church for three years. Presently, he is Dean of the Martin Luther King, Jr. International Chapel, Morehouse College, Atlanta, GA.

Weptanomah, who had been trained as an elementary school teacher having graduated from Millersville State Teachers College (now, Millersville State University),

Millersville, PA, wore the role of First Lady graciously. She loved and supported her husband. She made sure the little ones were cared for and nurtured. She even learned to drive a stick shift Peugeot up and down the hills of Lynchburg. She was a blessing and a gift from God. My father often joked in her presence that she still had the first dollar she ever earned as a teacher in Lynchburg.

Early on, however, the new ministerial couple had to cross an interesting domestic bridge. My mother, Weptanomah, did not cook. She never had to. She never learned to. And she really wasn't trying to. On the other hand, my father had grown up with southern food quenching his appetite. Dining out and "take out" at that time, especially, weren't day-to-day options. Somebody was going to have to learn or make time to see that food would be on the table.

One day, recalls my father, he just wanted some biscuits with his dinner—homemade biscuits. Keep in mind that during the 1960's, wives were expected to cook. Not Weptanomah, though. If my father wanted biscuits he'd have to make them himself. This was a defining moment in my parents lives, not to the extent of their marriage being in jeopardy. Quite frankly, during that time, neither one even believed divorce to be an option. However, they were on the verge of letting the biscuits issue become a real stickler, proving that most domestic issues and arguments are precipitated by things that aren't always earth-shattering but rather negligible.

It was that day that my father decided not only would he make biscuits but he would also take the responsibility of cooking for his wife and subsequent family. In doing so, he diffused what was sure to be a lifelong issue of tension, giving relief to his wife who didn't like being under that meal-to-meal pressure, trying to do something she didn't like doing, nor had the skills to do, anyway. Her husband was a natural. He had the ability to see the makings of a meal in the refrigerator when no one else did.

His friend, Dr. Vaughn, a cook himself, recalls the frog legs and the muskrat stew that my father cooked. He humorously commented, "He was a great cook, but you never really knew what you might be eating." My sister fondly called his cooking, "meals-in-a-bowl." She learned to cook by watching our father. She tells that his greatest cooking lesson was to use her nose. One day while food was on the stove, unattended, she was coming towards the kitchen; he was in his study. "Daddy, do you want me to check the food?" she asked. He replied, "It's done, just turn the stove off." She was amazed. You see, he could simply smell and tell that the food was done. And so, for the forty-eight years of their marriage, when he was in town and not away preaching, he did the cooking… all of it.

He must have possessed supernatural taste buds as well. He ate just about anything and would enjoy it. I'm sure that I probably slightly annoyed him because I wasn't trying to eat octopus, goat, liver, or grass (or so it seemed to me). I picked him up one morning to take him downtown to the University of Maryland Cancer Center for treatment. He was by no means a regular consumer of fast food. He tried to eat balanced and in moderation. That morning, however, he said, as I helped him into my vehicle, that he'd like to stop at McDonald's and get a cup of coffee and a breakfast sandwich. No problem, I thought to myself. There was a McDonald's more or less around the corner. We could stop there, go through the drive-thru, get on I-695 East to I-83 South and get downtown in time.

As I started in that direction, he asked me where I was going, and I responded that we were going to McDonald's. He said, "Uh uh, go that way." "That way" was in the direction which would take us away from the beltway and inevitably mean that we would end up having to drive through the city, traffic lights and all. There was another McDonald's roughly four miles away from his house that he wanted me to take him to. "Daddy, it's McDonald's. Why this one?" "The sandwiches taste better at this one," he replied. Such were his supernatural taste buds.

As my sister and I grew, so did my mother's culinary repertoire. Pop Tarts and bacon or cheese toast (Not grilled cheese sandwiches... there is a difference, you know.) was our standard breakfast. Baked chicken, boiled potatoes, and canned lima beans was our standard dinner meal. The other was hamburger goulash on toast. Then, without getting too far ahead, Libbyland Kids Meals were introduced during our pre-teen Baltimore days. They were essentially TV dinners for children. Once or twice, our parents hired a housekeeper, but that never lasted for any length of time. Momma and Daddy had come to a resolve and it worked. My sister and I are, today, living proof of the same.

Marriage is compromise. It is hard work. It is about sacrifice. My parents, our parents, were great. In my opinion, our home-life was better than most of those whom we grew up with. I looked forward to having my friends meet my parents and visit our home. Thank God that my father decided to make those biscuits. By doing so, a wonderful and blessed union was able to move forward, ultimately lasting until the day my mother passed in 2006.

There are no words to adequately describe the way in which my mother dealt with her diagnosis of cancer and the subsequent time that God gave her to be with us. For me, however, the best I can convey is that she was as beautiful in her dying as she was in her living.

The sense is that she may have known about her condition some time before I or my sister did. With regards to my father, I can't speculate. I can say, however, that at the point of his awareness, he could not have been more loving, caring, and dutiful, tending to her every need.

The day my sister and I were informed that her condition was terminal was like no other. A few days after, my father and I were with her in her hospital room. He asked her who she would want to preach her funeral. She looked to her left where I was sitting close by her bedside and said, "Mann (my nickname)." I knew that my father had preached both his father's and his mother's funerals. He'd also preached his brother's funeral who had died in 2004. Now, that mantle, though no desire of mine, was falling on me.

Theirs was, in many ways, a Christian marriage that became a model for any number of young women and young men to hope for, as well as for any number of couples, new and not so new, to emulate. There was no doubt that they had love for each other. They both believed that God had brought them together. And they had mutual respect. I've not known them to be overly or openly affectionate, but the signs of their devotion and adoration were without question.

Although my father spoke of his naivety, having come from Selma, my mother was to some degree sheltered and found herself away from home for the first time when she went to college, which was all female and predominately white. She had little exposure to black culture. Her personality, however, allowed her to become who she needed to become in given situations, and she certainly possessed mothering skills and wit. Once, when I was rebelling about participating in an endeavor that would ultimately prove beneficial to me, she told me with motherly emphasis, "Mann, just fake it." Initially, I didn't want to remain at the college I felt I'd been coerced to attend, especially since it was predominantly white. I took her advice, given the context at that time that she wasn't asking me to be hypocritical. She was, in some way, speaking from experience, and in another way sharing advice that sometimes in life we have to smile when we don't feel like it, but in time we will. On more than one occasion, I've heard my father say, "Your mother is a smart woman."

What made their marriage work, in addition to the God-factor, based on my reflection, was the fact that my mother "knew preachers." Having grown up as a preacher's daughter often going with her father on preaching engagements, having been around her father's preacher-friends and preacher-colleagues, and having been influenced by her mother's involvements in the church, as well as her mother's involvements in Ministers' Wives conferences, etc., were invaluable experiences in "cutting her teeth" for the kind of ministry-marriage in which she would find herself. She could relate, and she could "talk church." My father loved that about her, and that was a major source of connectivity. Many mornings and many nights, I would hear them when waking up, when trying to go to sleep, or at the kitchen table, just talking and talking about what was going on religiously and/or socially in the lives and ministries of those with whom they were associated. That kind of free banter brought a certain pleasant atmosphere in our home.

Their connection at this level would give rise to what is relatively common today in church-life: "team ministry." My mother was not a preacher, and she (as far as I know) had no desire to preach, let alone be called. Nevertheless, by today's standards, given the invitations and opportunities that came her way to speak or facilitate workshops for women, she would quite frankly be considered a minister. Yet, she was okay being who she was as the wife of my father and First Lady.

It was only a few years after my father accepted the "call" to become the third pastor of the New Shiloh Baptist Church, after seven years in Lynchburg, that my mother would retire from the Baltimore City Educational System altogether in order to give that much more of herself to her family and to her ministerial involvements. "One dreary October day, I was sitting in the classroom and just couldn't decide what I was doing there, so I left and never went back," she said in an interview, referenced by Jacques Kelly of the *Baltimore Sun* newspaper.[3] Early on, she continued her music ministry, playing for the Gospel Chorus and subsequently the Revival Choir in New Shiloh, that is, until her "boss" fired her. He (my father) told her that it was time for the church to move in a different direction. They would both smile about it. During the 1970's and 1980's she authored several books, with (sshhh) "ghost writer help" from my father. Most notably was *The Black Minister's Wife*, which even today serves as a classic guide for women who are married to preachers/pastors. It was and is also a good read for the preacher/pastor, too. In so many ways, my mother redefined the role of the pastor's wife. "We, as wives of God's servants, seek identity but it is not an identity found in ourselves or our husbands. It is found only in God," she wrote. [4]

My parents often traveled together, nationally and internationally, to various preachments, conferences, conventions, as well as for pleasure and "R & R." And, my mother had carved out a niche of her own, initially operating a thrift store for the church. She was the founder of the Progressive (Shilohettes) Shiloh Workers, a group which raised scholarship money for the church's high school graduates, among other things. She became an instructor of preachers at the Virginia Seminary and College of Lynchburg's extension school in Baltimore. She was the first woman to earn a Master of Divinity degree in 1975 from Virginia Seminary and College, Lynchburg, VA. She also took classes at the Howard University School of Religion, Washington, DC. At that time, a young man by the name of Walter Thomas had joined New Shiloh. Subsequently, he was called to preach and enrolled in the Howard University School of Religion. Often my mother would commute with him from Baltimore and back (my mother was not a highway driver). Now, the (then) Rev. Thomas was no dummy (as my father would say). He was above average in intelligence. However, there was a day when the commute home was silent because the passenger had received a higher grade than the driver.

What really, really put the "team" in ministerial team, however, was when my father was led of God to begin two radio broadcast ministries. Not only were they highly effective, due to their phenomenal coverage and could be viewed as being directly associated with the growth of New Shiloh throughout the 70's, but the two hour-long broadcasts: WCAO, "The Bread of Life," Sundays, 7:00-8:00 a.m. and WBAL, "The New Shiloh Worship Hour," Sundays, 9:05-10:00 p.m., gave my mother a platform to be featured as the announcer for them. Every weekend, my father would dutifully write her script for the opening, the sermon introduction, and the closing of the broadcasts. Then, my mother would record those scripts live during the services with her inimitable voice. Given New Shiloh's incomparable Music Ministry, the spirited worship and prayer(s), and the anointed preaching (of one who many said, upon hearing, "sounded like Dr. King") and rounded off by uplifting words from the First Lady, gave rise to a tremendous package of evangelistic fervor and became a model for any number of other broadcast ministries. People from as far away as Nova Scotia and the island of Bermuda were being blessed by this husband and wife team, especially via WBAL's (then) 60,000 watt station. It was truly a game-changer.

Naturally, my sister and I were coming of age during all of those years. Our home-life was sound. Yes, there were times when I felt somewhat restricted. My friends seemed to have more freedom than I, but as I was constantly told, pertaining to the rules and regulations of 3501 Sequoia Avenue, "It's for your own good." I truly enjoyed being a preacher's kid (PK) and I believe that goes for my sister, Weppy, as well.

Perhaps, the previously mentioned classic axiom of "opposites attract" can be applied to my parents, but deeper still was that scripture was affirmed in their marriage. "Two became one" as spiritually they'd been equally yoked. I've heard both of them say what I've previously mentioned, and that is that marriage IS hard work. This they had experienced because nothing good, strong, and lasting occurs without tests, challenges and sacrifices. But I look with 20/20 hindsight at their years together and am inspired that love does conquer all, even when it comes to who's going to make the biscuits. "Opposites may attract," but I'll add that opposites that attract can be sustained and can endure by the grace of God. Attraction is one thing. Staying together is another. "Toots" and "Wepp," as they respectively and affectionately called each other, stayed together.

# 3

# The Gospel of "It's Yours"

---

As the new year of 2016 began, those who'd gathered at New Shiloh for our Annual Watch-Night Service had come to the service, at my request, dressed in formal and semi-formal attire. We had risen from our knees having "prayed out the old year and prayed in the new year." We were rejoicing in the celebratory moments of the calendar having changed, by the grace of God. Saints were hugging, shaking each others hands, blowing whistles, blowouts, and squawkers, including myself. It was festive and jubilant as praises were also going up and anticipated blessings for the new year would be coming down.

I'd left the pulpit to hug my wife, Monique. Joining her on the front row where she sits were, among several others, Rev. and Mrs. James and Loretta Thompson. Rev. Thompson is the retired pastor of the Nazarene Baptist Church in our city. Having been licensed, ordained, and installed by my father, over thirty-five years ago, he'd spent time under my father's pastorate first as a member, then a deacon, and was called subsequently into the ministry.

As I concluded embracing my wife and was trying to go back into the pulpit, Mrs. Thompson, with a broad smile, caught my attention and pointed to her husband. "Do you recognize anything?" she asked of me. I was somewhat perplexed. Pastor Thompson looked good in his black tuxedo and, quite frankly, I wasn't making any connection with what she was asking of me; that is, until she pointed to his contrasting white, formal tuxedo vest. Then, I understood (although admittedly, I didn't recognize it). I put two and two together in that brief moment, and with an elated smile and response to both of them acknowledged that my father had, indeed, once worn that vest and had graciously given the same to Pastor Thompson, who, after over three decades, was proudly wearing this gift from his pastor.

I can still recount from my teenage years being with my father on numerous occasions at church, conventions, revivals, and other like settings receiving compliments for the unique style of ties that he wore. "It's yours, Doc," I would hear him say to colleagues and laypersons alike. Given the first opportunity, for example at the end of the service, he would take his tie tack off, loosen his tie, pull it from around his neck and say to the happy recipient, "It's yours." Subsequently, over the years, I cannot count the number of times persons have approached me, telling me how surprisingly blessed they felt when they were given ties, shoes (like new—and often brand new), shirts, suits, cuff links, and other items by my father, who took great pleasure in sharing, giving, and being a blessing to others.

He had a tremendous self awareness over the years of his life that the God who had blessed his parents in Selma, the God who had made a way for Black people (as he called them), the God who had provided and made a way for him, especially during his formative days in ministry pursuing his seminary education, and the God who was opening doors for him, having come of age, had been good to him, and he had no cause to be selfish. In fact, his philosophy of giving was rooted in the belief that: (1) God was going to take care of him and his family, and that (2) giving was one of the best ways to be blessed by God.

He embodied that Southern hospitality of greeting others and giving of himself. It was nothing for him to have guest preachers or "sons" in ministry come to our home, cook for and feed them, which he took great pleasure in doing. Then, at their departure, give them a book or two, or some memento that he'd picked up during his travels abroad that was precious to him (and quite frankly us, his family) and, yes, several ties and so forth.

He was fond of putting "something" in the hand of children, college students, and families. Personally, it was a happy expectation seeing his handwriting on an envelope when away at school, because there would inevitably be a check enclosed. He never left his sisters or sister-in-law, grandchildren, nieces, or nephews without "blessing" them. And, he probably was the one who first said, "Get yourself some ice cream," when doing so.

Stewardship is an interesting concept. I have come to the conclusion that it can effectively be taught and practiced. However, more often than not, it is innate and, simply put, a way of life. Some people have it. Some people don't. Harold Alphonso Carter had it. And if you stayed around him long enough, not only would you see it in action and be blessed by it, but you, too, would seek in all likelihood to emulate it. Practically everyone I know who has been impacted by his giving and giving spirit has, in turn, been inspired to do the same.

This stewardship concept is, therefore, demonstrated beyond gift giving. It affirms the sovereignty of God. It includes the giving of time. It includes the giving of help or helps. It includes the giving of wisdom and advice. It includes the giving of presence, not just presents. It includes the giving of talent or talents. My father could easily be seen as being a giver in these proceedings as well as aspects that I have not cited.

He gave himself as a husband and a father. He gave himself as a servant of God. He gave himself as a friend and confidant. For example, one of his "sons" in ministry said to me, since his home going, "Just think about all of the secrets he took to the grave (about each of us)." And, truly, he gave himself as a preacher and pastor, most notably the almost fifty years at the New Shiloh Church.

Having been led of God to call the congregation of New Shiloh to build a new state-of-the-art, multimillion dollar church—something that during the late 70's was unheard of for an inner city African American congregation—the leaders generally caught the vision and, as referenced in Nehemiah 4:6, "had a mind to work (build)." The historical records show that, when New Shiloh broke ground to build that, the church only had about $25,000.00 in the bank. However, the leadership was setting the example of faith, and the majority of the congregation were claiming the vision. There did come a time, though, when there was a work stoppage and the construction crew was nowhere to be found having received no recent pay. The church's then-Business Consultant, Dea. Leonard Coleman, got word to my father who was preaching in another city. When he learned that the church did not have the necessary cash on hand to keep the work moving forward, he called home to speak with his wife.

That Sunday, when he arrived at church, he put nine $10,000.00 checks in the hand of the church's then-trustee, now Chairperson and Church Business Consultant, Dea. Donald Lee, who turned the same over to Dea. Coleman that day for immediate deposit. My parents had, in mutual agreement, decided to take a mortgage out on their home and gave the same to the church.

My father rarely talked about or spoke about giving or stewardship. Instead, he practiced it and demonstrated it. I recall once getting a glimpse of his annual tithes and offerings statement that the church issues to all members who use the envelope system. I was profoundly moved, even at the age of about twelve or thirteen that anyone could or would give that kind of money to the church. That glimpse helped tremendously in shaping and affecting my own stewardship, as an adolescent, from that moment forward.

Not long after the thirty-one-year-old Rev. Donté Hickman had been called to pastor the Southern Baptist Church in our city, he had come to the Baptist Minister's Conference, which holds its weekly sessions each Monday at our church in the Harold A. Carter Chapel. Following the session that day, Pastor Hickman came to my office before leaving, as we are good friends.

Having grown up in Baltimore, as well as having been called into ministry when he was seventeen years old he, like numerous other young impressionable preachers, he took advantage of having the opportunity to attend New Shiloh and hear Dr. Carter whenever he could, as well as spend time with him whenever possible. Dr. Carter had, after almost sixty years in ministry, over 130 "sons and daughters" in ministry as the direct result of his ministry. However, he had many, many other men and women who'd come into ministry who claimed him as a mentor, surrogate pastor, and confidant. Such was Rev. Hickman.

Rev. Hickman often tells of one of the conversations that he had with Dr. Carter, during his formative days in ministry, having come to appreciate his ministry as the Revivalist for the Gillis Memorial Community Church, where he had been licensed to preach by his pastor, Dr. Theodore Jackson. Following one of the revival services, Rev. Hickman asked Dr. Carter if he could come by his office at the church some time to get ministerial direction. Dr. Carter, with his topcoat already on, having sweated from that evening's preachment, took his tie off and handed it to the young preacher and said to him, "Sure."

It wasn't long before Rev. Hickman made good on his request. He recalls that it was a Saturday afternoon when he saw Dr. Carter's car on the church's parking lot at the new location on Monroe Street. Unannounced, he worked his way in only to find Dr. Carter hanging pictures in his new office.

As the conversation commenced, Dr. Carter said to this youthful sponge of a preacher words he'd often say: "First of all, you need an education. If you believe you can do well with liberal arts courses, then that's the kind of school you want to go to… Don't feel like you need to go where everyone else is going… Find a school where you can expand your capacity to think." Rev. Hickman indicates that Dr. Carter went on to ask him, "Who are your role models… influences?" Rev. Hickman was silently saying to himself, *You are, Doc.*

I share this aspect of their encounter that day because, again, giving is more, much more, than the giving of things. My father's gift, among others, was the gift of counsel. He gave advice, wisdom, and guidance to so many who have commented that his discerning words were timely, accurate, and of God. To be sure, I'm not aware of any counsel that he gave anyone that proved erroneous. He possessed an uncanny intuition that proved to be right rather than wrong.

Before, Rev. Hickman left, he'd been given two of my father's books: *The Prayer Tradition of Black People* and *The Preaching of Jonah*. He'd also been given a copy of his 25th Silver Anniversary Journal. All three items, Dr. Hickman cherishes to this day.

Fast-forward about fifteen years. (The now) Dr. Hickman

was in my office following the minister's conference. Again, he'd come into my office, which was connected to my father's. When we heard him come in, we went into his office to speak. He had another preacher, who would be one of those who claimed him as a surrogate father in ministry, with him. After a few pleasantries and brief reflections on the sermon heard during the conference that day, Rev. Hickman noticed an electronic shoe buffer. My sense was that Rev. Hickman had not seen one before. "Doc, this is nice," he said as he pushed the button to see if it was in working order. To my amazement, my father said, "Take it, it's yours." Even the other preacher was somewhat surprised.

Rev. Hickman unplugged it, wrapped up the cord, lifted it like he'd won the Heisman trophy and proudly exited saying happy good-byes, walking past me with that buffer that I'd given to my father a couple of years earlier for Father's Day. Yeah, I felt "some kinda way." I had my own in my office, which I subsequently put in his. After his passing, it still remains in the same spot, in the office that was his and now—do I dare say?—mine.

I learned that day that my father didn't always connect what he had with its earthly source. The point being, he wasn't necessarily emotionally attached to things. Without a doubt, he enjoyed many of the niceties of life, but he had the capacity not to be attached to them. It wasn't so much an "easy come, easy go" disposition; I truly believe he understood the love and even sacrifice engendered in what he was blessed to acquire, as well as what he was given. It was more like a "blessed to have, blessed to give" disposition. Such was an enormous part of who he was. In some way, he couldn't help it. He wasn't trying to impress, win friends or favors, or even unload that which he didn't want. It's simply that he had the gift of giving; a giver was he.

# 4

# The Gospel of Self-Inspiration

---

It was a hot, humid, drizzly, and overcast Friday; the 7th of June, 2013. My family, the New Shiloh congregation, along with numerous preachers, pastors, bishops and dignitaries gathered, en masse, at the New Shiloh Baptist Church for the Home Going of our beloved father, pastor, colleague, mentor and/or friend, respectively.

Ironically, the main sanctuary's air conditioning system "decided" to simply "age out" that week. We tried all we could to have it repaired and/or replaced, but given the limited time the best that we could do was to rent several industrial, commercial units which, quite frankly, only made a negligible difference. It was just one of those Baltimore days (weeks). Needless to say, I smiled within...I had to. I knew that my father would have been truly okay with the entire temperature situation. He didn't like air conditioning, in general. And he sought not to preach with air conditioning, if he could avoid it. The fact that it wasn't working was, for me, his way of humorously saying, "Guess what? I'm still here."

The service was, nevertheless, a splendid sight to behold and to be a part of. The deacons, ministers, ushers, greeters, staff, and choir members of New Shiloh looked grand and royal, truly befitting the somber yet celebratory occasion. Many preachers and pastors, from across the country, cut short their attendance at the Hampton Ministers' Conference, Hampton, VA. in order to be present, inasmuch as the conference was held that week.

Personally, it's never been my practice to look at bodies, but the staff of Vaughn C. Greene Funeral Homes, P.A. had done a tremendous job with my father. He looked as he, a man of God, should. He had shared with me his desires, and he had even written some plans in his will. Needless to say, I had the formidable task of having been asked by him, during more than one conversation, to do his eulogy. By God's grace, I sought to celebrate his life around the theme, "The High Calling of God" (Philippians 3:14).

I found it to be quite interesting and even a little disappointing that of all the sentiments I shared during the home going message I gave for my father that what one of our city's local newspaper reporter's chose to include in his article were the few words spoken regarding my father's good taste and not the many words spoken about his ministry. For decades, the media and, to a great extent, the entertainment world has sought to exploit the connection between ministers and things of value and prestige.

Almost without question, when reporters want to know about the ministry of the church, the interview will begin with, "What is your church doing to help the poor in your community?" "Tell our audience about your Food Pantry." "How many persons come through your Clothes Closet and how often is it open?" It is as though their only perspective of the Church is its (her) relationship with the less fortunate. I hasten to add that, without a doubt, the Church is called to help provide for those who are without: widows, orphans, the homeless, the mentally ill, those suffering, etc. However, the Church, as I understand its (her) existence, should not be held accountable solely on its (her) prioritization, or lack thereof, of helping the poor. Simply put, helping the poor is only one of the important ministries of the Church. The Church and therefore its (her) leaders and members are called to a variety of ministries, but it (she) has but one mission: to seek and to save those who are lost/unsaved. That's the priority. If the media wants to know how the Church is doing, let them start with evangelism. Let them hold us accountable for winning people to Jesus Christ or the lack thereof.

Nevertheless, theirs is to speculate, accuse, and/or create innuendo about where ministries and/or pastors live, what they wear, what they drive, and what they earn. For shame. They don't know that God honors faithfulness, obedience, and humility. They don't know that God promises the abundant life not just for those who serve as leaders but for those who seek to live for Him and carry out His Will. They don't know that God blesses generationally, often in spite of a previous generation's faithfulness or unfaithfulness.

Although I am not professing or espousing prosperity preaching in its popular form, I am professing and espousing what I have seen and witnessed in my own experience and walk with God, and in this case, especially as it relates to my father (who, incidentally, was far from being a prosperity preacher in its popular form).

Still further, I as the writer and you as the reader know all too well the stories from the Bible up to this present day of those who've sought to use the ministry for personal gain and the inevitable downfalls associated with them. Hustlers and charlatans always appear where money (and often property and vulnerable people) are found.

However, there is more to the understanding of prosperity than the acquisition of stuff. So, I have taken the time to assert the preceding disclaimer, of sorts, because even Jesus appreciated and was even blessed by things of value, even to the—do I dare say—exclusion of the poor. We are familiar with the narrative of Jesus having been invited to the house of Simon the leper in Bethany. While there, a woman came in "having an alabaster box of very precious ointment, and poured it on his [Jesus'] head...." (St. Mt. 26:7, KJV). We read that the disciples became indignant and viewed the woman's act as wasteful because, from their perspective, the ointment could have been sold and the money given to the poor. Jesus' response was one of deep appreciation for what the woman did and then He made this declarative statement: "For ye have the poor always with you; but me ye have not always" (26:11).

When we are blessed and when we seek to use our blessings for God, as well as know where our blessings come from, we are honored/favored by Him. It has much to do with stewardship. It has much to do with prioritizing and recognizing God's sovereignty. It has much to do with sacrifice. Money and material things are wonderful, but only in their context. Specifically, money is just a means to an end, but in and of itself, there's nothing inherently wrong with it. It is the attitude that many have about it that consumes them, corrupts them, spoils them, and too often, ruins them. That's the problem. It's when "the gotta-have-its" take over. Let us seek to properly understand and quote the Apostle Paul's words to his spiritual son, Timothy: "For the love of money… the love (lust) of money… is the root of all evil: which while some coveted after, they have erred from the faith, and pierced themselves through with many sorrows" (1 Tim. 6:10).

I was mindful that so many who had come to pay their final respects to my father and their respective friend, colleague, teacher, mentor, pastor, and loved one had been influenced by, or at the very least had an appreciation for, my father's love of life. He genuinely and truly enjoyed life: his family, his home, his ministry, and so forth. Uniquely, he was able to possess the abundant life that his Savior promised without any hint of trying to impress or be seen or accused of conceit. To the contrary, he was respected and appreciated for his way of living…his style, his persona. Frankly, not too many (pastors) could live as he did, during the time that he did, have what he had and still be admired, appreciated, and loved. But as Dr. Vaughn told me, "There was so much he could have been arrogant about with his many gifts and talents, but he wasn't, and that's why God blessed him."

Jaguar vehicles were unheard of, especially in the Black community, but my father owned two of them in the 70's: a vintage white 1957 and a green 1973 XJ6. Once, in an effort to applaud my father's humility, one of the deacons said publicly that his pastor didn't need to drive around town in a big Lincoln or Cadillac. He simply had no idea what a Jaguar was. In 1974, my father observed his tenth pastoral anniversary at New Shiloh. He (we) drove to his anniversary banquet in his newly acquired 450 SEL silver Mercedes Benz. That same year, he took us (his family) to Bermuda where I watched him barter the price of a yellow gold Rolex Datejust in one of the island's premiere jewelry stores. Having been influenced by Dr. King, Jr., he wanted to have a watch like he had. Examine the iconic photo of Dr. King, Jr. with his hand up to his head, taken at the age of thirty-five when he received the Nobel Peace Prize in Oslo, Norway, or several other photos, and you will see on his left wrist nothing other than a yellow gold Rolex Datejust. Even Rev. Jesse Jackson sought to follow suit, as I'm sure many others did as well.

One could not go into his church office/study without admiring the intricately hand carved exotic wood desk, which he had shipped from Panama, along with a matching chair. Many have sought to find a similar desk for themselves but to no avail.

It is worth noting that my father gave me permission to drive to my senior prom in that white 1957 Jag, which looked like a classic baby Rolls Royce, with my prom date and now wife of over thirty-one years. Unfortunately, that car was totaled, one weekday, when my father was rear-ended by a Volkswagen Beetle while sitting at a red light at the intersection of Liberty Heights and Wabash Avenue in the city while on his way to church. Once rear-ended, the force pushed him forward into the back of the car in front of him, sandwiching and subsequently cracking the frame of the Jag. No one was hurt except me. I was to receive that car upon graduating from college. Fortunately, I still have the chrome Jaguar hood ornament that I salvaged.

During the summer of 1979, after I'd graduated from Baltimore Polytechnic High School, my father graciously asked me to accompany him on a nine day missionary journey to Romania. He had come to meet, and was subsequently invited by, one of the Baptist leaders of that country, Dr. Jon Bunachu, during a previous Baptist World Alliance Conference. As we traveled throughout parts of Romania, even spending several days close to the Hungarian border, churches and halls filled to capacity and beyond, as people came to hear the African-American, baptist preacher from America. One church was so crowded that the baptismal pool was opened in order to make more room for people to stand in.

The people were so hungry for the Gospel that a two hour sermon was not adequate. I was not in ministry at that time, but Dr. Bunachu insisted that I would bring a twenty minute greeting during each service, usually two each day. My father always felt that it was that experience that watered the seed of a calling in my life, especially given the fact that whatever I said during those greetings was extemporaneous, (and according to him) insightful, and inspirational.

When it was time to return home, our host, Dr. Bunachu, dropped us off at the Henri Coanda International Airport. During the time of our visit, Romania was a communist country. It remained such until its revolution in 1989. When we got to the security counter, a guard was seated behind the same and never once looked up. We handed him our tickets and passports but for whatever reason, he would not stamp them. He was saying something, but without an interpreter we could not understand him, nor could he understand us. No one else seemed to be of any help. Of course, we had our luggage, and I was carrying a beautiful burgundy 5"x 7" Persian rug rolled up under my arm that my father purchased during our limited downtime. During one of our visits to a church, we were introduced to a pastor who obviously spoke Romanian but also spoke German. Fortunately, I had taken German as my foreign language for four years, during high school. To my father's amazement and sheer delight, I was able to interpret the conversation between my father and that pastor. Given my father's schedule, especially during my high school years, I really don't think he was aware, to any great extent, that I'd come to learn German, in some limited way; at least, at that time to be able to rudimentarily communicate.

It was in the same family of reactions that I got from him when he learned that I made the "fresh/soph" (9th grade) football team at Poly, or when I'd won the MVP award for tennis at Eastern. It was a mixture of being proud, being pleasantly surprised, and asking himself, *Where have I been?*

I'd spent most of my boyhood days playing pick-up baseball

and football down the street from our home, on the lawn of, what was then, Our Lady of Lords Catholic Church and playing basketball in our backyard, where my father had put up a backboard and goal. Yet, somehow, those after school hours, Summer days, and Saturday afternoons never really translated, in his mind, to his son being able to play organized sports and be half-way good at doing so.

As previously written, he spent a lot of time outdoors as a boy himself, but because of his somewhat small size he wasn't always the first picked for the sandlot (as he called it) team. His was to enjoy more individualistic recreational sports, like tennis, bowling, ping pong (which he was quite good at, even winning a tournament, trophy and all, in seminary) and, of course, fishing.

Occasionally, he would come outside in the backyard to play basketball, but that two-handed, chest shot of his was so old school, before old school was old school, that it made me and my neighborhood friends lovingly tease him. Bottom line, he really wasn't that athletic. He bought himself a ten speed bicycle, when they were all the rage, and we went riding. He could hardly get back to the house, having become winded, trying to peddle up Edgewood St. We laughed and laughed, but only after he'd fallen over on our lawn, bicycle and all. He took my sister and I out on a rowboat at Loch Raven Reservoir (if my memory is correct). My mother had the good judgement to stay on the shore. He rowed us out on that lake pretty good, but we thought we would never get back. It was a little scary but mostly hilarious. He was sweating like he was preaching.

He loved all kinds of sports, especially boxing. He was a

true fan of Muhammed Ali. As a collector of African and African American art, he had two powerful pieces of Ali: a portrait and a glass statue of "the Champ."

He never, though, sought to even slightly live vicariously through me. Perhaps, there's a little bit of something in me that wished he had. However, I've rationalized and attributed, perhaps idealistically, his somewhat hands-off support, regarding sports, to his seeing a bigger picture of what God would do in my life. I knew it wasn't meant to be, myself.

Nevertheless, I figured I had nothing to lose, so I said something in German to the guard, explaining our visit and that we really needed to get through in order to check in and catch our plane. He must've understood because still, without looking up, and believing that my father was praying, the guard picked up the stamp and processed our passports and paperwork.

When we arrived at the Frankfurt International Airport, in Germany, our layover window was very tight, which we knew would be the case. However, we literally had to sprint (reminiscent of the old Hertz Rental Car, O. J. Simpson commercials) in order to get to our connecting gate. All the while, I was running with that rug and my carry on.

By the grace of God, we made it to the gate, sweat and all. It is the Persian rug that is actually the focus of my sharing about our Romanian missionary journey. When we returned to the states and, subsequently, to New Shiloh, my father placed that beautiful rug at the foot of the pulpit. From 1979 until 2011, having been brought from the former location to the new location, my father preached at New Shiloh, along with all others (myself included) while standing on that rug. The only reason it was replaced was because someone decided one day that it would look better in their home or that they could benefit from its sale. Needless, to say, it was a wonderful memento of a father-son pilgrimage in a foreign land that truly bonded us closer together and gave us something to think about whenever we stood at the pulpit to share the Gospel of Jesus Christ.

When I graduated from college and was simultaneously called to pastor my first church in May of 1983, my father gave me that Rolex that he had purchased in Bermuda as a gift. It blew my mind. Hmmm… my oldest son is graduating from seminary, soon. You needn't ask (smile). The answer is, "of course." If I have the hood ornament, you know I have the watch.

I truly believe that whatever giving spirit I have is the direct result of my father's actions, as I witnessed them, as well as having been told about them. He really didn't want anything in return, either. Granted, he enjoyed receiving gifts, but his great joy was making others happy, starting at home. Hardly ever did he go anywhere to preach without returning with an outfit, or two, for my mother. Holidays and birthday were always exciting because we never knew what he was going to give her, or us, for that matter.

His selection of gifts was fascinating, to say the least. He once bought and brought me a complete stereo system built into a black, hard shell briefcase. The lid split into two speakers. The inside (bottom) housed a turntable, cassette player, and an AM/FM radio. It was electric and battery powered, so I could actually carry it like I was a fourteen-year-old businessman. The likelihood is that gift had much to do with me eventually having my own short-lived DJ business in high school and my first two years in college.

As I cite the *Baltimore Sun* newspaper reporter, Jacques Kelly's, quote from my eulogy for my father, I trust that it will be received now in its proper context. Indeed, it was Kelly's closing part of his article entitled: *New Shiloh's Rev. Dr. Harold A. Carter Sr. remembered at funeral*:

*He also recalled his father's style: If anyone has enjoyed life it was Harold Carter. He was eating Häagen-Daz ice cream when the rest of us were eating Sealtest. He walked on other people's carpets in alligator-skin shoes. He drove a pea-green Jaguar when people in Baltimore didn't know what that car was.*[1]

About twelve years ago, while the two of us were driving in his black Volkswagen Phaeton W12 to the Hampton Ministers Conference, held annually the week after the first Sunday in June in Hampton, VA, I asked him, "Daddy, what accounts for your good taste? Where does it come from? You were buying bottled water (Perrier) from Eddie's in Roland Park way before buying water was a trend." I went on to elaborate: "Your parents and upbringing were relatively modest. It seems to me that you've been able to raise the standard." I was hoping, of course, for a direct response, but like my father would do on many occasions, he talked around my question. His response was vague enough that I made a mental note in that moment to myself: he's not going to give me a direct answer; I don't even think he really knows.

One of the self-analyzing observations he made of himself was, "I'm an enigma to myself." Most often, he used that analysis when referring to his preaching and the effectiveness of his ministry, a thought which we will come back to later in this book. He really felt that he was not worthy and that he hadn't done anything to have warranted the way in which God used him. He couldn't explain it. He didn't try. He just went with it.

Now, as his son, permit me to attempt, notwithstanding my own response to the question I asked of him. I do know that like most in the Deep South, African-Americans, regardless of their means or status, weren't affluent with regards to tangibles or material things during the days of my father's upbringing, albeit with a few exceptions. Nevertheless, generally, they were affluent with intangibles: a belief in God, a strong family life, a loving home, a desire for higher education, and so forth. In other words, coming out of slavery, and during the days of segregation and pre-Civil Rights Movement, our people had a drive to better themselves and achieve a better life than they were born into. I dare say that, in some way, there was a quest to achieve "the American dream." In this same vein, I would add that such a generation also had in mind to make the world a better place, and even more importantly, to leave the world a better place for their sons and daughters.

Following the educational path of Dr. King, my father did his seminary studies at Crozer Theological Seminary, 1956-1959, outside of Philadelphia, PA. He often spoke of one of the professors, Dr. J. Pious Barbour, who had more than tremendous influence and impact on his life, calling him "a Black theological Aristotle." He appreciated greatly the endless hours that he, along with other seminarians like his great friend, Dr. William A. Jones, Jr., spent with Dr. Barbour in his home outside of the classroom. Although Dr. Barbour's "campus home" wasn't much to appreciate, it was what he poured into my father that was the real appreciation. He was one of those rare influences that had the ability to bring out the best in others.

A colleague of mine, Bishop Jeffrey Reaves, pastor of the Good Shepherd Baptist Church, Petersburg, VA, once said to me after hearing another of my father's influences, Dr. Samuel Dewitt Proctor, whom I was privileged to have as my D.Min. Mentor: "Every time I've heard Dr. Proctor preach, I've left wanting to do something." Indeed, there are those who have the ability and gift to inspire others to rise above their circumstances, go beyond the norm, and take legitimate action. Given the influence of his parents, both of whom had "put something" into all five of their children not to accept mediocrity, the mentorship and nurture that Dr. Barbour had on my father was, without question, extremely valuable, letting him and others know that with God he could stretch his mind, make a difference, and think big.

That influence, in my opinion, not only was lived out in my father's pursuit of education, his prayer for and claim of a beautiful wife, and his manifested vision to be a blessing for the glory of God, but that influence materialized (pun intended) in his lifestyle pertaining to his style and good taste.

Void of ostentation, my father was "metro male" before the term existed. He was always dressed in a three-piece tailored suit (his colleagues begged him to reveal his source, which he rarely disclosed. I can say that he and my mother periodically traveled to Montreal, Canada. Subsequently, packages would be delivered to the house.), custom French cuff shirt, unique rings, a gorgeous tie, fine shoes, over the calf socks, a chain and pocket watch (which he designed along with his tie tack), and his "Determined" medallion worn hanging from a gold necklace around his neck. Of course, he never went anywhere without a choice briefcase or shoulder bag. Traditional. Classic. Timeless. Words fitting and descriptive. There were days, I must say, that it seemed as though he went down the buffet line of his wardrobe arbitrarily. He could put together combinations I could never get away with, but somehow only he could make them work. Then, there were the impeccable topcoats: cashmere, fur, fine linen and cotton, as well as his wide variety of hats and caps. He was never outside without one or the other, mostly due to his obsession about have something on his head. He always felt like he was fighting a cold, so protecting his head and throat was essential. I cannot tell you how deceived he felt when, in 1976, Listerine was forced by the Federal Trade Commission to admit that its usage to fight germs was false advertising and for naught. He regularly kept some kind of cold pill in his vest and bathrobe pocket (Triaminic was his favorite for years), and some type of antibiotic was essential. He's the only person I've ever known who would take a portable heater with him when staying in a hotel. Admittedly, with the exception of the hats, caps, and the daily wearing of suits, his son I am. God knows it seems as though I'm constantly on guard against the slightest tickle in my throat.

Soaps, colognes, and surrounding himself with niceties, in general, gave him a certain "lift." I contend that it wasn't easy pouring himself out in ministry; preaching almost daily for years, pastoring, preparing, and traveling, takes it toll, not just physically, but mentally, emotionally, and spiritually. Such things were his way of bolstering himself, and probably in some existential way, they became his uniform, his armor as he "fought the good fight." When he was working on his doctoral degrees he would smoke a pipe, but that proved to be a passing phase. Since he wasn't given to any other vices—certainly nothing habitual or addictive, he found a certain inspiration in being good to himself. Countless times, I heard him say, "You can't preach to others, if you haven't preached to yourself first." And, preaching can come in different forms.

From the foods he enjoyed to the places he traveled and from a simple shoeshine to a good book, my father's ultimate aim was to declare the glorious Good News of the Gospel of Jesus Christ. I've seen him go without certain creature comforts without complaint, so I know that he wasn't dependent on them. His was a greater dependence. Yet, he sought to carry himself a certain way as a representative of the Kingdom and to set an example for others, especially in one's decorum and attire. For him, every day was Sunday, and his was to refute and take the high road over and against the desire of cultural trends to dumb down and/or dress down standards, customs, and attire.

I once listened to a eulogy by Dr. Gardner C. Taylor of a California pastor whose name was Dr. T. M. Chambers. It was recorded on cassette tape by my maternal grandfather, Dr. T. Robert Washington, who pastored the Second Baptist Church, Germantown, Pennsylvania. My grandfather would go anywhere by bus, train, car, or plane to hear and record a good sermon. His tape collection was incredible.

Dr. Taylor said of his colleague and friend, Dr. Chambers,

something that arrested my spirit. He said, "He was a preacher every day." I borrow such a profound line and without hesitation use the same about my father. He was a preacher every day.

# 5

# The Gospel of Adventure and a Pioneering Spirit

Over forty years ago, New Shiloh had a regular newsletter publication called *The Shiloh Echo*. In 1974, the June edition was given over to my father's ten-year pastoral anniversary. In a section titled, "Profile," which was a brief synopsis of my father's and the honoree's ministry, he was quoted as saying, "If I am not involved in something meaningful and creative, I would die. This is what gives me a creative restlessness."

As previously mentioned in the first chapter of this work, such a drive and determination was put in him early on in his life by his mother. "From my mother, I gained a drive to get ahead, to excel, to be dissatisfied with mediocrity," he wrote. He also gave credit to the strong influence of Dr. J. Pious Barbour, Dr. M. L. King, Jr. and the spirit, in general, of the

Civil Rights Movement that collectively spoke to his spirit to "be somebody," to dream big and believe for big things. Moreover, he believed that, in turn, he owed it to others to inspire them to do likewise or, at least, to involve and position them in such a way that they would experience greater things.

It is no wonder then that, as a young idealistic preacher and pastor, when his eyes fell (the exact time and place I cannot recall) by happenstance, as some might say, or by providence, as others would say, on a church's portable, lighted marquee citing across the bottom, "Determined To Work For Jesus," such words would resonate deep within his spirit. He innately knew that given the right time and place those words would embrace the kind of church and ministry he would like to have.

Long before we knew the term "life coach," my father was the embodiment of one. God had gifted him with discernment, intuition, self-motivation, the ability to motivate, and an uncanny wisdom to respond to the questions of others about the vicissitudes of life in ways that seemed to be accurate and proved inevitably to be beneficial.

Bishop Walter Thomas asked me over twenty-five years ago, as we were discussing effective pastors, including my father, "Who do you know in ministry who has made few, if any, mistakes?" Both of us understood the fallen nature of humanity, that no one's perfect. However, he was making the point that, given my father's track record regarding decisions he'd made in ministering, again and again he proved that he made right choices and that his advice could be trusted.

When his ability to see not just the big picture but the essentials and components combined with his innate drive to move beyond the norm, all the while praying and seeking to be Spirit-led, such allowed him to be the initiator of much that addressed God's Kingdom, here on earth, through his own ministry, as well as through the ministries of others he'd given counsel to.

He attributed much of the effectiveness of his ministry, especially as it relates to New Shiloh, to a moment of inspiration during a Sunday service in early 1979. Mindful that the church had embraced the persona of a traditional Baptist congregation in polity, structure, and doctrine, he knew that he'd been blessed by a strong deacons ministry (then, board). Such men—as they were at that time—like Sidney Johnson, Bernard Jones, Anderson Turner, Moses Knight, Noah Jordan, G. Leonard Coleman, Sr., Alonzo McLeod, Willie Greene, and Willie Simms were stalwart, God-fearing men. However, the sense was, given the rapid growth of the ministry and the influx of educated, professional young adults and their families, that the deacons ministry was still a necessary one but that it would need to be infused with new life for the next generation and beyond… and not just new life but a new look. The image of twenty or so senior men sitting at the front of the sanctuary dressed in black suits was slowly seeing its day coming to an end, that is, if the church was going to continue to grow and keep the many new persons who were joining.

So that fateful Sunday, Pastor Carter came out of the pulpit before the benediction and walked up and down the aisles of the sanctuary pointing at various men and women saying, "I want to speak with you. I want to meet with you." No one had any idea what he wanted. Some were even fearful that they were in some kind of trouble. When he was done, he returned to the pulpit having a list of sixty names, indicated when he desired to meet with those he'd pointed out, and gave the benediction. That day, a revolution of church leadership began in the New Shiloh Baptist Church.

Careful not to offend any of the official church family (deacons, deaconesses, and trustees), the first group of Stewards of Christ was birthed. These hand-picked men and women soon came to find out why their pastor had called them out:

*You have been called together for the specific purpose of studying deeper demands of what it means to be a Christian. You have been called to be a group in the church living on the cutting edge of Christ-likeness; putting into practice many of the things we give lip service to but little action. You could easily be trained to be deacons or trustees; but this would defeat the purpose. We do not want to go this route because, all too often, the offices to which we are elected become far more important to us than the services we are called to render. We need, in New Shiloh, a solid core of Christians who seriously commit themselves to following Jesus...*[2]

This inaugural meeting, led by the pastor, went on to call each one to make a verbal commitment to the following 10-fold discipleship emphasis:

1. Daily Devotions
2. Family Life Enrichment
3. To Tithe and Give Liberally
4. To Witness and Render Service
5. To Render Personal Evangelism
6. Fullness of Spirit
7. Faith Adventures

8. Mutual Love
9. Responsibility and Punctuality
10. Church and Pastoral Loyalty

These men and women were personally taught by my father for a year. Many of them are now preachers and/or pastors. Others are what he called lay-ministers, like Dea. Elbert Sloan.

It is #7, Faith Adventures, that claims our attention for this chapter. In my father's manual for disciples, *Building Disciples In the Local Church*, he explains "Faith Adventures" by asking the following questions: "What burden do we feel for Jesus Christ? Are we going to be quick to say 'we can't do this. The job is too big'? Is the job too big to witness Christ in a crime-infested community? Is the job too big to call a whole city to revival? God's people must be willing to face failure in order to succeed. Remember, we seek not to please people; we seek to please our Lord!"[3]

Faith Adventures was not just a point of emphasis for Pastor Carter. It was not just rhetoric. It was not simply a principle to be emphasized. It was personified in his ministry.

Having been used of God to serve as the evangelist in crusades in many parts of the world, like Kenya, Bermuda, Montreal, Germany, Romania, Panama, the Philippines, and Venezuela, as well as any number of places here in America, it just made sense that he would be led to call the city, where he ministered, to Jesus Christ. He had already started the unusual work of serving as the evangelist for New Shiloh's own revival, preaching six consecutive days (including Sunday) in his own pulpit. Having first started in the month of January, eventually the revival was moved to the end of the summer. This meant that the New Shiloh Church family was being challenged to remain energized and faithful during a time of the year when most church-congregations and pastors are vacationing and enjoying a little R & R, as they were preparing for The Summer-Ending Revival Crusade, a crusade that in some ways has become legendary. People of God literally attended the crusade as their summer vacation. Personally, I cannot begin to convey how much energy and sacrifice it takes for a pastor to preach his or her church's own revival... and be the worship leader, as was the case in New Shiloh. But, think about it. Who better knows the spiritual pulse of the people than the pastor? Who better knows what the people, youth, and adults need than the under-shepherd?

And, so, having been raised up and established by God as an anointed evangelist, it seemed only right to call the city of Baltimore to Christ. On the strength of much prayer, planning, and preparation a local African-American congregation led by her spiritually courageous pastor went to the Civic Center in downtown Baltimore and witnessed 14,000 persons attend an evangelistic crusade in June of 1978. A little as two years later, as a new decade dawned, it was done all over again under a theme that I actually worded: "Entering the Eighties With Christ." My father would often acknowledge that little piece of history, but he also loved to tell how I drove all over the city (having been old enough to drive) passing out fliers, handing out free, promotional tickets, and putting up placards and posters wherever it was allowed.

Regarding renting out the Baltimore Civic Center at a time when such was unheard of for a local church, his friend, Dr.

Vaughn, comments, "He was way ahead of his time." Such was something for the Billy Grahams or the faith healers like Oral Roberts to do, not a traditional Baptist Church. But in 1976, my father led the clergy and laity alike to (then) Memorial Stadium, where 20,000 gathered for an Easter/Resurrection Day Sunrise Service, and with the conviction of member and deacon Larry Young (also a former state senator) an unprecedented three-day Crusade was held at the multi-million dollar new home of the Baltimore Orioles, Camden Yards, in October of 1992, where my father along with Dr. Frank M. Reid III, pastor of the Bethel A.M. E. Church of Baltimore, served as evangelists. Note that not long after I returned to New Shiloh to serve with my father, I, along with Dr. Jamal H. Bryant, pastor of the Empowerment Temple A.M.E. Church of Baltimore, served as evangelists, as Larry Young once again helped pave the way for a return to Camden Yards in September of 1997.

There were church and community-wide marches. There were pilgrimages to the Holy Land, Rome, Kenya, and Egypt, among other places. There were 24-Hour Prayer Vigils, mentoring programs, and the establishing of the Carter Children Center, which was coordinated by my mother, where community youth could attend after school for tutoring, crafts, recreation and snacks, and the list of services and ministries goes on.

Three innovative schools have been founded because of the ministry's big thinking and creative vision: (1) The Saturday Church School has existed for forty-three years and is still the primary source for Bible Study and training for members of all ages; (2) The Carter School of Music, (recently renamed) has existed for 25 years and has been faithfully served by Dea. Alethia Starke, Executive Director, where persons of all ages acquire the highest level of voice and/or instrument training, and (3) The Harold A. Carter Determined Biblical & Theological Institute, has existed for 20 years and was founded to give affordable seminary training to clergy and laity alike, as long as the applicant has a high school diploma or the equivalency thereof.

Although it's easy to take for granted, but the vision to build a state-of-the-art, multi-million dollar church facility, if nothing else, was a Faith Adventure. To think that an urban congregation with little money in the bank, as previously mentioned, could get financing originally in the amount of $9 million dollars, in the 1980's, was an adventure in and of itself. That amount would soon grow to $14 million dollars. And, then, because of the leadership and faithfulness of the members, to see the mortgage eliminated and the note burned in 2002 was truly a blessing and a God-ordained victory.

And the adventure didn't stop there. In 1999, the church was led to purchase approximately six additional acres that abut its present property. This acreage was the Cloverland Dairy, but when the company decided to relocate, the church purchased the same for $650,000.00, definitely under market value. Incidentally, that amount was per my suggestion. Having acquired the same property allowed for much needed additional off-street parking, as well as made buildings available for child development, businesses and even an 82-unit senior living facility (new construction). All of this development is known as The New Shiloh Village (a CDC).

Dr. Johnny Golden who served as my father's assistant during the years, 1986-1994, and is presently the pastor of New Unity Church Ministries in Baltimore, MD, indicated that one of the hallmarks for him regarding my father's ministry is that he can be credited for sparking the development of the west side of Baltimore. Our church's C.P.A., Dr. Arnold Williams, has intimated the same for years that as Pastor Carter felt led to build in what was an area of urban blight, revitalization has come in many ways, like the renovation of Mondawmin Mall, the expansion of Coppin State University and the new construction of the Center for Urban Families.

I tend to believe that, generally, we want to be around work and projects that prove successful and effective for the glory of God. I also believe that a lazy church is a dying church. I once heard my father's mother, Dr. Lillie Bell Carter, say during a casual conversation about church-life that church members always need something to do – some project, something to challenge and stretch their faith. Indeed, long before she made her comment, it had already been written, "Where there is no vision, the people perish" (Proverbs 29:18a).

New Shiloh has been able to mature spiritually and be blessed because she has had a pastor who has not been ashamed to stretch himself in faith nor unwilling to stretch the congregation's faith. Yes, there were doubters and naysayers along the way. They're always there, albeit thankfully and usually in the minority. But even then faith must be strong enough to prevail and preside over negativity and adversity.

One of the major hurdles that my father faced that

ultimately brought tremendous solidarity to the ministry was his desire to break the traditional Baptist roles of women in the church. In addition to the integration of his wife into the ministry in non-traditional ways, he sought to incorporate women into the leadership of the church at an entirely new level.

Pastor Carter's spirit of inclusion has to be seen in context. Again, not only was he a product of the south, but he was a leader in a faith rooted in thousands of years of patriarchal history. Nevertheless, not long after coming to serve in New Shiloh, he saw to it that the church provided funds for a young woman who had demonstrated a deep commitment for Christian education, namely, Brenda Johnson (now, Greene). With the church's financial support, she matriculated and graduated from Howard University's School of Religion, Washington, DC, and was subsequently hired as the church's first female Minister of Christian Education a position she held for eleven years, full-time. It was said of her, by my father, that through her ministry women and men were forced to see more in faith besides Sunday worship, prayer meetings, and funerals. She was able to begin the process of seeing the faith as a necessary tool for youth (development), adolescent problems, marital (relations), stewardship growth and general discipleship. The legacy Mrs. Brenda Greene left in the church was a new openness and support for multiple Christian ministries.

In many ways, her ministry paved the way for another female who'd grown up in New Shiloh and saw Mrs. Greene as a mentor, namely, Robbin Blackwell. Robbin accepted her call into the ministry in 1982. She went on to complete her seminary training at Wesley Theological Seminary. She was brought onto the staff in January, 1996 to serve as the Minister of Ministries, which she did for approximately twenty years. Presently, she is the dean of the Harold A. Carter Determined Biblical & Theological Institute, as well as one of the seminary's professors.

One of the more radical moves that Pastor Carter felt led to make, however, was where the official board or boards were concerned. Based on the biblical definition and understanding of the word deacon and over and against the commonly accepted biblical precipitous for deacons, as believed to be found in Acts 6 (where we know the word "deacon" is not found), but we do find that seven men were called upon to assist the apostles, my father, espoused that the work of a deacon is the work of a servant. Of course, traditionalism and sexism had come up with the word deaconess to give women, mostly wives of men who were deacons, a title and place; albeit, subordinate to the men, who were deacons.

In 1983, my father recommended that all, including the deaconesses and the trustees, should be known and understood to be servants, hence deacons. This was no easy pill to swallow. Even some of the women could not grasp the concept, initially. However, the recommendation was soon accepted and the rest is history. Today, it almost seems antiquated visiting other churches and find that distinctions are still being made between deacons and deaconesses. Even versions of the Bible have been updated to be inclusive and avoid chauvinism.

Oh, but he didn't stop there. At a time when it was unheard of, when the death of the then-current chairman of the deacon board occurred, Pastor Carter recommended that the next chairman would be a female, namely, Deaconess Elizabeth Adams. Needless to say, this would be groundbreaking. Nevertheless, the recommendation was approved, and Dea. Adams served until her self-initiated retirement for twenty-two years and is now Chairperson Emeritus at the wonderful age of ninety-five.

As we were planning our trip to Seoul, Korea, which has been previously referenced, my father suggested that, since we would be in that part of the world, we might as well go to Beijing, China, and Hong Kong. As fate would have it, we were joined during our tour of parts of Beijing with another pastor from the states and a couple from England. I only recall that the pastor's last name was Lucas—Dr. Lucas. I remember hearing that he had passed several years ago, through one of the leaders of the Progressive National Baptist Convention, of which he was actively involved.

The five of us toured that day, climbing part of the Great Wall, visiting Tienanmen Square, seeing the giant pandas at the Beijing Zoo and Aquarium (including Ling Ling, before she was given as a gift to the Veno Zoo in Japan), and taking in one of the famous acrobatic productions. It was during the intermission that I truly got mad at my father for the first and only time in my life. And, it was essentially over nothing. He had an interesting way of not carrying anything if he could help it and if someone else was around to have them do the honors. It was just the way he rolled. Those of us who knew him, knew to expect that he had no problem handing off anything so that he would be free and unencumbered, even if it was a matter of a few feet.

Well, during the intermission, the two of us went to the gift shop at the pagoda-style venue. It had been an exhausting day and this was our final destination before returning to our hotel for the night. We'd already climbed the Great Wall, and when we came down from the portion we'd ascended, he'd commented that his legs were shaking uncontrollably. We all laughed on the tour van and he soon fell asleep. I'd caught him napping during the first half of the production, so I knew he'd probably had enough. Anyway, there we were in the gift shop and although I hadn't nodded off, I'm sure I was a little weary, and having been together all day, we probably needed some private downtime. Both of us purchased a few items. I recall that I needed some film (yes, film) and then I could see it coming. I knew it was coming. I could hear it coming. So, having been first to make my purchase, I put my little bag inside a shoulder bag I had with me and I headed for the exit. Just at that time I heard him say (and I was too close to act like I didn't), "Doc, put this over in your bag." *You mean to tell me, you can't carry that little bag of knick knacks yourself?* I thought to myself. When we returned to the auditorium we sat several seats apart, but I digress.

At some point, during the course of that day, Dr. Lucas asked my father, "Dr. Carter, what's the secret of your (ministerial) success?" That caught my attention. I wanted to hear what his answer might be. He thought briefly, perhaps ten or fifteen seconds, took a visible breath and said, "Well, Doc, I'd like to think that I'm a hard worker." Dr. Lucas nodded his head.

Quite frankly, I'd never associated the pastorate with the utilitarian sense of hard work. But it can be, and in many ways it is. Effective pastoring is unattractive, behind the scenes hard work. It's work that most people don't see. It's visiting and counseling. It's praying and preparing. It's administering, writing, and reading. It's being on call and working when others, including family members, are able to enjoy the holidays. And, if one wants to truly be a blessing and advance God's Kingdom here on earth, one cannot afford to be lazy or hands off. One has to put the hours in over and beyond Sunday services and a weekly Bible Study. One must be imaginative and creative. One must be convicted in one's soul. One must have an inner drive... and inner fire. One must let one's light shine, the world will see the good works, and God will get the glory.

*...To know him was to want to be better and to push harder.... Dr. Carter helped me develop an authentic unwavering ministry ethic. He made all of us want to be better.... In my life, I know his influence was like a flood. I have never seen (anyone) so committed to serve the Lord and who totally enjoyed it. (He) was a pioneer in operating outside of the box.... He was out of the box. In fact for him, the box did not exist. Tradition had its place, (but).... He taught and showed everyone that God is the one who gives us dreams, ideas, and the power to make it happen.*[3]

In the year 2001, one afternoon my father came into my office and sat down. "Doc," he said, "You know this year is about over. What do you think about 'The Burning Bush' as our 2002 church-wide theme. I believe it's a theme that will further motivate us, especially in the area of evangelism. Also, next year will be our 100th anniversary." Having found much joy, personally, in the Moses and Exodus narratives, I was wholeheartedly in agreement and indicated the same to him. "Let's go with it." We prayed and "The Burning Bush" was our 2002 church-wide theme.

In an effort to create a spirit of celebration for the church's centennial, he proposed to me the following idea: "Let's do a 30-day revival on 'The Burning Bush' during the early Spring. One of us will preach every day (evening) with the exception of Mondays and Saturdays about the burning bush. We don't have to get hung up on a crowd. I just believe that once folk know we're serious and committed that the wind (the Spirit) will be at our backs. I'm not even gonna get hung up on the choirs and all that. We'll just preach and believe God for a great benediction for the church. I do think, if you're in agreement," he went on to say, "that we will suspend all meetings and rehearsals and just focus on the Word."

I felt a big WOW in my thinking, and I'm sure I gulped a breath or two before responding in the affirmative. We quickly got busy promoting the 30-day Crusade with fliers, billboards, radio ads, etc. And, throughout the month of March 2002, "The Burning Bush" Crusade was held. By the time we came to the culminating service, the church had caught hold of the spirit of what was taking place and the momentum was such that there was more than an enthusiastic desire to keep the crusade going. I couldn't help but think back to one of the songs I learned as a boy during summer camp at Camp Pineridge for Boys, in New Hampshire, entitled "Pass It On." The song begins with the line, *It only takes a spark to get a fire going, And soon all those around can warm up to its glowing...*

As the year unfolded, the church had, yet, another Spirit-filled Summer-Ending Revival Crusade, the week after the 4th Sunday, in August. After the first summer's revival having joined my father in pastoral ministry, in 1996, we alternated preaching for the same. I always felt and believed that the revival was "his baby" and his to do. However, he genuinely seemed to appreciate the two of us kind of tag-teaming; and deep down I was honored to do it.

In my opinion and in so many ways, my father was the spark as well as the embodiment of the fire. He not only was blessed to conceptualize but was given the anointing and abiding favor of God to carry out the same. No wonder several of his "sons" in ministry, especially Dr. Charles Booth, Dr. Tommie Jackson, Dr. Major McGuire, and Bishop Walter Thomas, affectionately nicknamed him, "the 8th Wonder of the World."

Note: *The Burning Bush: Revival Crusade Sermons*, Carter and Carter, Jr., Gateway Press, 2002 is a publication of sermons preached during the 30-Day Revival Crusade and is available at www.newshilohbaptist.org

# 6

# The Gospel of Dr. Quick-Prayer

The reality of and the likelihood is that opportunities and moments seized for prayer were far greater and more numerous than opportunities and moments when there was no prayer. I think that makes sense. In other words, my father prayed at times when most of us didn't. He prayed pretty much all the time.

You and I might pray in the morning, upon rising from our sleep. We might pray before we eat our meals. We might pray before we go to sleep at night. We might pray in the event of some circumstance that might arise. And, we might bow our head to pray when it's time to pray during the course of corporate worship. I know we don't want to admit it, but even when we say to someone, "I'm praying for you," it's more of a cliché than an intentional act.

My father, who attributes his formative prayer life to his father, once writing in his 25th Pastoral Anniversary Journal, "From my father, I gained a great reverence for prayer.... Still further, he wrote: "Nathan Carter (his father)... provided a rich fund of Black prayer insights as he pastored Black people.... He often told his family that prayer was the foundation of his life and the key to all of his accomplishments."[1]

He seemed to pray in order to pray. Once we parked on the lot of Sinai Hospital on our way to visit a member. Before we got out of the car, he put his hand on mine and prayed that our visit would be effective. Then, having come to the close of our visit with the member, of course, we held hands with the member and the family members. He gave me "the nod," so I prayed only to be followed by him giving a closing prayer. It was prayer on top of prayer.

I've been with him when he's led in prayer before going fishing, before going on a plane, after the plane has landed, as soon as he's turned the key having purchased a new car while still on the lot of the dealership, after taking me and a group of my friends, as teenagers, bowling, during and at the close of any family function (with immediate or extended family members); he prayed for the right wife; he prayed for the conception of his children and their (our) subsequent good health. It was nothing for him to pray for those who'd come to visit and pray for him when he was fighting for his life and close to death. And rather than saying to people, "I'll be praying for you," he prayed for them, then and there. (I think you get the picture; yes, that he prayed all the time.) And, you will want to know, his prayers made a difference in our lives and the lives of others. He prayed, and he had power in prayer.

Once while on a summer family vacation, as was our custom whenever the vacation was over a weekend, we went to church. I do not recall where we were, nor do I recall the church we attended. I do, however, recall that as our family sat in the congregation that the pastor recognized (or got word) that my father was there. Following the pastor's sermon, he called on my father to give the closing prayer at the altar. When the service was over, my sister and I walked outside to wait at the car (presumably, a rental, as I seem to recall) for our parents. Two of the female congregants walked by, not paying any attention to us. "And who was that man who prayed. Where did 'pastor' say he came from?" asked one of them. The other responded, "God sent him. That's where he came from." I was a pre-teen at that time, but the words of those women, as they passed by have been etched in my memory. They had been blessed by the prayer of "this visiting pastor."

During the 1970's, my father's seminary *alma mater* formed a Black Church Studies Program at Colgate Rochester Divinity School, Bexley Hall, and Crozer Theological Seminary. Twenty prominent pastors from across the United States were invited to participate with the aim of each one receiving his Doctorate in Ministry degree, as mentored by Dr. Henry H. Mitchell. Dr. Mitchell is quoted as having written, "We have Harold A. Carter to thank for using the program to facilitate the capture of the (prayer) tradition… And he may be thanked also for being the living bridge between the oral and written cultures—the authentic product, himself, of the tradition he records, while having acquired the additional identity of the writer/reflector/scholar."[2]

Over the three years of the program, my father acquired a more formal knowledge and appreciation for the historicity of the prayer life of his people. Ultimately, his final dissertation was edited, tweaked, and published bearing the title: *The Prayer Tradition of Black People* (Judson Press, Valley Forge, PA, 1976). One significant part of the program was having the students/pastors spend six weeks in West Africa, doing research on their respective projects. It was during this experience that one, single miraculous moment occurred, wedding the project of my father's to the African culture he was in. It has, over the years, become legendary.

I was privileged to have the gist of this incident retold to me via a telephone conversation for the purpose of accuracy regarding this writing by the inimitable Dr. Wyatt Tee Walker who witnessed the miracle, first hand. The same was subsequently corroborated by Bishop John Bryant. The M. L. King fellows were on their way home after six weeks in West Africa, along with some of their spouses (my mother, included), Rev. Tyrone Pitts (now, Dr.), their guide, and Dr. Henry Mitchell. They had left Lagos, Nigeria, by bus and were en route to Kotoka International Airport, in Ghana. As they were traveling, their bus broke down. The driver tried all he could to get it running again but to no avail. The group was stranded on a road where traffic was slight. One or two cars passed but obviously the group needed a bus for them and their luggage. Finally, a broken down jitney came but was filled with locals and even a few chickens. That driver tried to help fix the bus, but it still wouldn't restart. The group asked him to see if he could send back help, but they weren't that hopeful, as phones were scarce.

It was then when my father said, "Brothers, it's time to pray." The group had already grown anxious because an hour was turning into two hours and getting to the airport in time to catch their flight was starting to be in jeopardy. Dr. Walker said humorously that one of the brothers, a Presbyterian pastor, said, "We don't need prayer. We need a mechanic." Notwithstanding, my father gathered the group in a circle just off the two lane road, they got down on their knees on the dirt shoulder, held hands, and he prayed for the group to be able to get to the airport in time to catch their plane.

Not long after, to the amazement of most—not all—a practically brand new empty bus was seen coming towards the group. Dr. William A. Jones, Jr. stood in the road until the bus came to a stop. "Sir," said Dr. Jones to the driver, emphatically, "We need your bus." The group transferred the luggage, boarded the bus, which incidentally was air conditioned—a real luxury at that time and in that area of Africa—and made their way to the airport in time.

From that moment on, Dr. Jones, Jr. gave my father the nickname, Dr. Quick-Prayer, which the rest of the group took to affectionately calling him. An interesting aside is that since they'd met in seminary and had become the best of friends, Dr. Jones had previously nicknamed my father, "Moon," because of his round head/face.

That answer to prayer occurred when my father again was

doing research for his doctorate in ministry (D.Min.) degree. With regards to his Ph.D., which overlapped to a great extent with his D.Min. work, he found that prayer, once again, paid off.

He was in the writing stage of the Ph.D. program at St. Mary's Seminary, Baltimore, MD, meaning that most, if not all, of the classes, research, tests, and surveys were behind him as his concentration was on systematic theology. He'd been invited to be the revivalist at the Ebenezer Baptist Church, Rocky Mount, NC, where Dr. Thomas Walker was/is pastor, a revival that he did for a number of consecutive years, as well as myself in subsequent years, when I pastored in Petersburg, VA. During the week of revival, he stayed in a local motel, in a first floor room. Having gone out one of the evenings to the service, he returned to his room to find that his room had been broken into. It seemed that someone, or some ones, had gotten in through the window of his first floor room. Fortunately, he had those things of any material value with him and on him: his watch, rings, etc. However, an attaché case was stolen. Probably, since it was locked via a combination code, the burglar our burglars took it as opposed to opening it on the spot. What it contained were the documents associated with his Ph.D. work and the draft of his dissertation itself. I'm sure at that moment and time, he felt that his work was of more value than what he may have had on in terms of jewelry.

Therefore, having reported the incident to the motel management and recognizing that statistically most petty burglaries go unsolved, even though the police came and generated a report, early the next morning he took it upon himself to do his own investigation. He quizzed one of the housekeepers, whom he learned lived in the general area. Granted Rocky Mount is not that large of a city. Most people do know or are familiar with one another. The housekeeper was able to point him in a possible direction. Now, please understand that my father by no means had any semblance of an aggressive personality when it came to worldly confrontations. His advice was to, "take low, be passive." Once, I told him how I stood up to a man who tried to bogard a parking space that I had a right to first, and he chastised me with voice unraised, telling me that people can be crazy, and I had no idea what the man may have had in his car.

Nevertheless, his years of research were all in vain, if he didn't take action. There were no PC's. He had no backup files. What he had... and all he had was in that case. Having been told where to go, he set out on a quest but only after he'd gotten up off his knees at the side of his motel bed. Then, he started walking through the neighborhood. Anyone he would see or pass, he would tell them who he was, what had happened and ask them if they knew anything.

Finally, he came upon several young brothers sitting on the steps of a home. He had that feeling that if he told them how important those papers were that they would be the ones to come through. And, so, he pleaded his case, and may have even offered a reward. They never said, "yea or nay," but later that day, without the briefcase, his papers and dissertation were found on the counter of the front desk of the motel in the lobby.

The prayer influence, boldness, and audacity has truly been

an integral part of New Shiloh's ministry. In fact, although my father brought to New Shiloh his own evolving vision of prayer it must be noted that New Shiloh began as a prayer meeting in 1902, with just three persons present. The prayer meeting had as its agenda the desire to seek God's guidance as to whether a church should be founded.

Early on, the young pastor began a monthly prayer breakfast for men. On average, about twenty men would meet on Saturdays before each 3rd Sunday, in the month. Two young men would also attend—myself and the son of Deacon Calvin Phillips; namely, Larnell, who is now Bishop Larnell Phillips and pastor of the Shiloh Temple Tabernacle of Prayer Deliverance Church, Zebulon, NC. Usually, the two of us went for the breakfast part and would slip away if there was a speaker or Bible lesson to make and fly paper airplanes in other areas of the church. However, it still proved to be fertile training ground, being around older, praying men, especially since both of us ended up in ministry.

On several occasions, as a boy, I would awaken on Prayer Breakfast Saturday mornings and wake my father, reminding him or asking him, "Isn't this Prayer Breakfast Saturday?" as he was almost oversleeping.

After about ten years of the Monthly Men's Prayer Breakfast, my father shifted the breakfast to be inclusive. I think it was the result of a Women's Day Prayer Breakfast one year that led to such a decision. Nevertheless, the Monthly Prayer Breakfast Fellowship now averages around 200 persons, often 300+, given the occasion. It has been going strong for over 40 years and is now under the general oversight of our Saturday

Church School.

In addition to the traditional Wednesday evening Prayer Meeting, a service my father inherited when he assumed the pastorate of New Shiloh, a small group of seniors began meeting for a one-hour prayer service on Fridays, at 12:00 noon. This service was essentially led by the church sexton, Dea. Willie Powell. In many ways, it was that prayer service that became the seed for the Daily 6:00 a.m. Prayer Service. The 6:00 a.m. Prayer Service was additionally heavily influenced by my father having been to Seoul, Korea, in 1990. I was privileged to join with him, as he'd been invited to preach for the Baptist World Alliance, which met in Seoul. While there, we visited the Yoido Full Gospel Church, pastored by South Korean David Yungi Cho. At the church's height, it was the world's largest congregation, claiming a membership of 830,000 (2007).

One of the phenomenal ministries of Dr. Cho's was one that was actually birthed by South Koreans Christians known as Prayer Mountain and may have had its roots dating back as early as the 1800's. State religions opposed Korean Christianity and those who were being persecuted ascended nearby mountains during the early hours before dawn to fast and pray for their country. This they did, daily. The Korean Christians had a unique way of praying, in unison, as a congregation (*Tunseung-Kido*). Experiencing such can be breathtaking, inspiring, and life changing, even as it's done in regular services of worship. Needless to say, being a part of such a move of God, while visiting there, greatly influenced my father. When the New Shiloh church was transitioning to its new location, my father felt led to incorporate such a daily prayer service. Having entered the new location, 26 years ago, even to the time of this writing, not a single day has been missed but that someone has been on the grounds of the church, in spite of weather, holidays, etc., praying to God, at 6:00 a.m. To help such a movement exist, my father was led to convene a small group of persons to serve as a nucleus for the work. This group of Prayer Warriors is effectively led by a retired Maryland State Penitentiary Warden, Dea. Howard Lyles. Dea. Lyles has faithfully served this ministry, which allows attendees a time of personal prayer, corporate prayer, and a brief, closing worship, during which a lay person or a clergy person will give a meditative/inspirational message. Members and friends continue to come from near and far to be a part of this daily, early morning experience.

During the same period of time, my father instituted the Sacred Prayer Urn; its genesis is not known to me. However, the basic concept is that of having members, and all who desire, place in writing their prayer request and/or prayers of thanksgiving in the urn, which is kept on the Communion Table at the altar. Each service of worship, especially those on Sunday begins with the deacons and ministers forming a circle at the altar while two persons raise the urn which is prayed over by the pastor or a designated person. This act of prayer is an act of faith, even as the congregants hold hands during the prayer, as do those at the altar, touching and agreeing, believing that the presence of the Lord will bring to fruition the prayer desires of the faithful. Indeed, over the years, all kinds of victories, miracles, and praise reports have manifested, and we believe to be the direct results associated with this act of prayer. Any number of churches now have prayer urns, having adopted that which takes place at New Shiloh.

For many years, particularly during the time I was in my teens, when New Shiloh was still located on the corner of Fremont Avenue and Lanvale Street, my father initiated Family Prayer Night. Each household, single or family, was given a consecrated white candle to be lit in one's home, ideally on Saturday night as a means of preparation for Sunday worship. A person or a family was called to gather around the lit candle usually placed on the kitchen table, to sing, read Scripture, and pray. This we did weekly in our home. Even at the age of dating, it was expected that I would be present on Saturday night to participate in this home prayer service, which usually lasted about twenty minutes. As a teenager, it seemed like such an intrusion, but I'm sure it kept me out of trouble and without a doubt gave my life, as well as my sister's, covering. "It's prayer time," one of us would yell out knowing that our father or husband was already at the kitchen table most of the time around 9:00 p.m., with the candle already lit, singing by himself, until we joined him. The sense was that even if, for whatever reason, we weren't there, he would have still gone ahead with the service, alone. It was that important.

# 7

# The Gospel of the Enigmatic Preacher

What I'm about to tell you is true. I witnessed it and heard it with my own ears almost forty years ago, and I've never forgotten it. I'd gone with my father to a convocation service where he'd been asked to bring the message, which took place on the campus of Lancaster Bible College, Lancaster, PA (not to be confused with my *alma mater*, Lancaster Theological Seminary). For whatever reason, I did not go to record for future radio broadcasts, but I sat on the second row in the center section of the auditorium amidst any number of predominately white faculty members and students. A few African-Americans were present, and they were guests, having heard via the church's radio broadcasts that Dr. Harold A. Carter would be the preacher on that day for that daytime service. Several such persons were seated directly behind me.

When my father finished preaching in the midst of that academic environment, as was usually the case, the Spirit was high and most of those who'd assembled were standing on their feet, including myself. Amidst all of the rejoicing, replete with "Amens" and "Praise the Lords," my father turned from the lectern to go to his seat, having concluded his message. "Smoke" was everywhere. I took a quick glance behind me just to get a visual of what was going on, and a typical African-American "mother of the church-type woman," still wearing her overcoat and looking like she could cook a mean sweet potato pie, standing about 5'2" and somewhat stout, blurted out, "That m——r f——r sure can preach." *Did she just say what I thought she said?* I asked myself. I was done.

Certainly, I would hope (with much different vocabulary) that those who've heard the preaching of Harold A. Carter, at any season of his ministry, have had similar enthusiastic reactions. It was an amazing moment to witness, be blessed by, and know that God was yet speaking through human vessels. I kid you not; his preaching was an event. African-Americans, whites, Protestants, Catholics, young, old, Hispanics, Jews, business people, military persons, Pentecostals, Fundamentalists, and so on were affected and blessed by what God did through him, whenever he stood to declare the Gospel of Jesus Christ.

Several days into writing this chapter, a woman who attended a funeral at our church (I believe she was an evangelist) came to speak with me as I was leaving church about to get into the cortège, as I'd just finished doing the service. She said, "I'm so glad I was able to catch you. I just had to tell you how much your father's preaching influenced my life. There was one sermon, in particular, that I think about all the time. I know I heard it over 35 years ago. It was called, 'I'd Rather Live In Stink Than Live In A Storm,' and it was about Noah having to survive with the animals, in the ark." Now, granted, it didn't really sound like a topic my father would typically come up with, but she was so definitive, and it had obviously stayed with her that I just had to rejoice with her. So much so, that I said to her, "I might have to preach that, myself." To which she replied,"I hope you do, 'cause I already have."

"Harold A. Carter," wrote Bishop Thomas in the previously referenced *Great Blacks in Wax* journal, "was a man for everyone. He was a preacher who had the uncanny way of making the message fit the hearer.... He was blessed to preach all over the world and, whether through an interpreter or on the native tongue, there was clarity to his communication and people always saw Jesus. He stood behind the pulpit and called all of us to a new life in Christ."[1]

People came to New Shiloh to hear Dr. Carter preach. No ifs, ands or buts about it. I emphasize this, because almost as effective as his preaching was his worship leadership. Most who experienced it would agree that no one could lead worship like him. Clergy and laity alike were awed and inspired by his energy to lead the entire service and still preach with anointing and power. He was the Praise Team, choir director, church clerk (announcer of events), liturgist, prayer warrior, sanctioner and cheerleader. He was a spiritual genius in ushering congregants into the presence of the Lord. "Put some energy into it," he would say in order to heighten the worship.

Early in the eighties, I overheard my parents discussing at our kitchen table an article that had to do with preaching. I had the thought then, that my mother saw her husband in that article, and my father thought that he could certainly identify with its contents regarding himself. Not long after their conversation and after they had moved on, I came downstairs into the kitchen from my bedroom only to find the article written by Larry Williams, left on the kitchen table.

*The Black evangelistic preaching style, like Black jazz and blues styles, relies more upon emotional urgency, rhythm, and spontaneity than upon any planned text or tone. The sermon is not a message but an "event." The "event" is the Holy Spirit's entering the preacher, his inspiring his words and lifting his voice to a power and intensity that no calculated histrionics could quite duplicate. Like a musician who is "in the groove," playing faultlessly, or an athlete who is "in the zone" and cannot miss, the Black preacher who has reached that certain level of inspiration becomes an instrument not only of the Lord, but of the members of his congregation, who finds their spiritual longings realized in the voice of the pastor. At his most sublime, the Black preacher, like the successful musician (and) athlete, may find himself (being used) almost unconsciously. To the unfamiliar observer, the cynic, or the nonbeliever, this process may look like grossly contrived or opportunistic showmanship. But to the congregation, as to the minister himself, the experience represents an authentic visitation by the Holy Ghost.*[2]

What a wonderful synopsis of the celebrative aspect of African-American preaching, as found in the traditional sense. I am certainly mindful that this aspect is still celebrative, but whereas it was once the preacher's alone to be used to lift the congregation with the help of the Holy Spirit, now the preacher invites the congregation to help him or her preach through the emphatic moments of the message and certainly to help him or her close. The "event" that Williams wrote about and the tradition of my father was to, in essence, stand flat-footed and flat-out preach into the celebrative moment. It wasn't, arguably, manipulated, contrived, or forced.

Such was the style of Dr. King, Jr., whom I've already alluded to as having been of great influence in my father's life and that of his preaching. Yes, my father, like most of us who preach, are amalgamations of those whose preaching we've been blessed by. My father acknowledged that his father, Dr. Jemison, and many of the preachers he heard in and around Selma, impacted his preaching greatly, even long before he accepted his call to preach. Black preaching has a way of getting in you whether you are in ministry or not. Indeed preaching, in general, should be that way. Given his early influences when he would accept his call, it was only providential that he would come into contact with one of this world's great preaching orators in the likes of Dr. King. Listeners of my father, live, via recordings or broadcasts often commented that they thought they were listening to Dr. King. The golden, tenor voice, the cadence, the articulation, the sense of scholarship, the resonance and "tuning up," the perception of preaching extemporaneously, (Frankly, such was not the case. Dr. King and my father wrote and prepared manuscripts. My father wrote out virtually every word in long hand, but seldom used or read from the same in the pulpit. Of further note is that a full viewing, for example, of Dr. King's *I Have A Dream* message at the Lincoln Memorial in Washington, DC, [1963] will show Dr.

King using his manuscript but at the point [shall I say] of inspiration he "left" the manuscript and moved into what seemed to be extemporaneous preaching. But we know that those words had to be more than just off the top of his head. They were crafted, written out and [based on recently found recordings] used by him before, during a message he had given at a high school), and for many years (where my father was concerned, until he shifted) the somewhat abrupt (to some) end to the sermon's climax, leaving the congregation wanting to hear more were some of the common threads they shared, albeit the influence came from Dr. King.

In addition to the aforementioned, it was a "black sage," as my father called him, by the name of Dr. M. C. Allen, who pastored the Leadenhall Baptist Church, in Baltimore, from 1937-1947, who arguably had the most significant impact on my father's preaching, especially once he was preaching regularly as a pastor. Dr. Allen was a contemporary of the likes of Gregory Hayes and Vernon Johns. He was a great educator, Bible expositor and a scholar when it came to "blackness" in the Bible. He espoused self-help and reliance, racial pride and faith.

When Dr. Allen resigned from the pastorate, he accepted the presidency of Virginia Seminary and College. Such was how he and my father, during his Lynchburg days, were able to cross paths.

Dr. Vaughn shared with me that Dr. Allen was an African American with Indian blood in him. He had curly, bushy hair (reminding me of pictures I've seen of Frederick Douglass). He preached everyday, during the chapel service, without notes and did so with amazing biblical insight and wisdom. Such was what stirred my father's spirituality, while tremendously influencing his preaching. My father wondered how Dr. Allen could have and convey such a wealth of biblical knowledge and share the same sermonically without having a manuscript in front of him, day after day?

At the same time, however, my father seemed to have developed his own "voice." He certainly wasn't imitating or mimicking. God had called him and the Holy Spirit was using all of his experiences and influence in forging him a unique voice unto himself. Soulful, insightful, natural, existential, homiletical, evangelical, and prayerful were major components found in his preachments. Above all, I've always found his preaching to be two-fold: 1. He was charismatic, without fail and 2. He was constantly searching for the Spirit, whenever he stood. I shared these two thoughts with him, and he seemed, with appreciation, to agree with my analysis.

It is a given that his messages were Christocentric. His was to always exalt the name of Jesus Christ. Sometimes I would tease him about his idiosyncrasies, one of which was his failure to remember names, or just simply mix them up. For example, he often called my sister (his daughter), Sue. Sue was the name of his youngest sister (whose birth name is actually Blanche). When I would tease him, I would always clean it up by saying to him, "But there's *one name* you've never forgot. Jesus."

Although he'd grown up around "whoopers," he wasn't one. When it came to "closing" his sermons, he was a "tuner;" and a sweet tuner, at that. Nobody could "tune up on" the words, "soon" or "early" like him.

His preaching bridged denominational and racial divides. He preached for services and crusades on military bases, home and abroad. During the 1980's and 1990's, especially, he regularly preached for the Assemblies of God, across the country. Who can forget that during the "heyday" of PTL, Jim and Tammy Faye Bakker had him preach for their television broadcast, twice? In1999, Coach Bill McCartney and Promise Keepers had him preach for one of their major crusades at the RCA Dome, in Indianapolis, IN.

It would be a natural extension, then, that his practicing of spiritual gifts would be heightened, particularly glossolalia and healing. I have been teaching a group of 35 young adults, who are disciples in training (for future church leadership), similar to the Stewards of Christ, as previously referenced. One of the men, John Coates, shared while giving his spiritual biography how he'd been diagnosed as having too much protein in his kidney. John said that when he approached my father, desirous of seeking prayer, that without any exchange of words between them, he reached out and put his hand on his lower, right side and said to him, "Everything will be okay." That was in 2009. John indicated that he felt something go through his body and ultimately had a sense of peace. Needless to say, he has not had that problem since.

From time to time, my father shared with me about how things, from inspiration for sermons to direction and vision for the church, were confirmed by the Holy Spirit. For example, after he had finished preaching for a Pentecostal "Camp Meeting" service, somewhere (as best as I can recall) in the Mid-west that the attendees were in corporate prayer. It was during the time that the new church was beginning to be built, and the burden was quite heavy on his heart. He didn't express this publicly. He left the stage to join others who were already praying in the Spirit, at the altar. Not long after he got on his knees to pray, someone stood behind him, laid their hands on his head and said to him, "All of the needs pertaining to the building of the new House of God would be met." He never opened his eyes. He simply received what was said and was resolved in his spirit that whomever the person was had been miraculously sent to encourage him.

Now, regarding the outcome and the results of his preaching, which is to say why people were so moved, blessed, edified, and most importantly, saved, why God opened the many doors that were opened for him, preaching in such a wide variety of venues, and why God would use him given his background of humble means were questions he often pondered about himself. Indeed, one of his own self-disclosures was that he was an enigma to himself. When it's all said and done, he seriously accepted the will of God in his life; that God was using him, in spite of himself and at the same time, because of he who was.

Who amongst us who claim the call of God can actually explain why? Why would God choose to use us, at any level? From Moses, to Jeremiah, to Paul, to Martin, to Harold and beyond, the "why me?" is in many ways an essential prerequisite for the preaching ministry. Then, when God begins to use us in ways that prove effective for His Glory it is a mystery and an enigma. Whether his own analysis, mine, or that of others one thing was certain. God was using his vessel and voice in a big way.

Undergirding the spiritual aspect evident in his preaching was a disciplined preparer for the preaching moment. He never, in my opinion, took his ministry for granted. He took his craft seriously. I know him to have had resources within arms reach, but usually he would sit at his desk in his home office with one of his choice fountain pens, a yellow legal pad, a King James version of the Bible and "get with God." More often than not, during the course of most weeks, he'd have some sense of what he would preach on the coming Sunday. I say this because he'd regularly cite his sermon topic in the Sunday bulletin which was typically printed on Thursdays, and no later than Fridays. He may have outlined or jotted a few thoughts or bullet points down during the week. And, it was nothing for him to take out his pen from his breast pocket and start writing on anything (wrappers, napkins, edges of newspapers, etc.) and anywhere. His was to always be open to inspiration and revelation. If my mother had one pet peeve about his ministry it was that he'd inevitably start writing during public outings, like banquets, concerts, and even during services when he wasn't preaching. Interestingly, he had no problem writing when someone else was preaching, all the while still paying attention, justifying it to her, saying, "Preaching inspires preaching." She thought it to be somewhat rude, and he would apologize, but he still couldn't help it.

Nevertheless, he would inevitably sit at his desk on Saturday nights, only pausing for family prayer, and write. And, because such was his pattern, there's no way that he could be accused of what we, as preachers call "Saturday night specials." He wasn't getting something together at the last minute. He was preparing, praying, processing, and preaching to himself. Literally, he had a way of being heard all over the house preaching to himself (I suppose, when things got good to him) in a voice and tone just above the sound of a whisper. He was often heard saying to other aspiring preachers, "How can you preach to others if you haven't been preached to or how can you lift and inspire others if you, yourself, haven't been lifted and inspired?" Before he mounted a pulpit anywhere, he'd already been in a pulpit of his own.

Such preparatory discipline was also evident in his preaching engagements outside of New Shiloh's pulpit. Generally, outside engagements allow most of us to repeat messages that "worked well at home." Granted, although he would write new sermons, he would still repeat, like most of us, but he would sit down and rewrite the whole sermon over as opposed to just rereading it. I still shake my head in wonder. But that was his way of "getting the message back into his spirit."

Those of us privileged to have listened to and watched him preach on a regular basis would have to agree that his delivery was not based on word for word memorization nor did he possess (as far as I know) the gift of a photographic memory. He was simply blessed to have the unique ability to write out his manuscript, read over it once or twice—sometimes during the service like while the choir was singing or the offering was being given then fold those pieces of yellow legal pad paper, stand behind the pulpit, read his text, and preach. For him, it must have been more about knowing his points, and more importantly, embracing the content of what he felt led to say all the while giving room for the Spirit to open up even further what he had prepared and even what he was saying, "in the moment." Such moments would build on each other until he'd sure enough, for lack of a better word "connect," at which point the congregation would sanction and celebrate the moment with him.

He would say to preachers on occasion, myself included, "you hounded that squirrel 'til you ran him up the tree." Such is what he appreciated in the preaching of others, of course among other things, perhaps because such had much to do with his own preaching.

Without a doubt, he loved preaching, and he loved preaching. In other words, he loved to preach, and he loved to hear and be blessed by preaching. Probably because of his southern upbringing, he had a strong affinity for Bible belt radio preachers. He was a genuine radio aficionado, so it was nothing for him to lay in bed late at night with those original yellowish plastic earpieces—not ear buds, earphones or headphones—we're talking the sixties and seventies, and search the dial on one of his short wave radios until he found such a preacher, either teaching or preaching "fire and brimstone." That was a huge delight for him.

He also was blessed by great whoopers like C. L. Franklin, Caesar Clark, and W. Leo Daniels. He also appreciated what God could do in the preaching of those who may not have had the best education, those whom he referred to as just "born preachers." And, he respected the stature and class of a Gardner C. Taylor and his dear friend, William A. Jones, Jr. From the seasoned preacher to his grandson, Daniels' first sermon, his was a sincere love of the preached word.

Although, like Dr. Barbour would do to him and his classmates, ripping their sermons apart, he would quite often do to me, although I want to believe that he found something in his son's preaching that blessed him as well. Based on the observation of many who watched him watching me preach (inasmuch as he generally sat behind me when preaching at New Shiloh, I could not see him, but I could hear him… most of the time… his silence was almost too much to bare) over the years they would convey the apparent delight, based on his expressions, in hearing his son preach. Yes, preaching in his presence was always intimidating, so there was nothing so affirming as hearing his sanctions while preaching and hearing him say, "Doc, you were prayed up, today."

I always felt that even when he was taking me through my post-sermon analysis (and, by the way, he loved to analyze: politics, people, world affairs, practically any subject… he was always well-read and informed) that it was his way of letting me know that no matter how well or effective we feel we may have done that we, in and of ourselves, never get it right. Up until the writing of this book, no one knows the following except me and him, but already having preached for ten years, in 1990, I compiled ten of my so-called best sermons and wanted to publish them as an anniversary commemoration. I asked him to read and proof them. To this day, that compilation is in a basement file cabinet. When he'd finished drawing lines through sentences, making notes in margins, and correcting this and that, well…

The reality is, my first published book, beyond the printing of two preaching booklets, *The Sacred Marriage—Getting Started in Pastoral Ministry*, (a title that he gave me, by the way) would probably be in that same basement file cabinet, having gone through similar scrutiny, except for the fact that I was a little older and my skin was a little thicker to "take it." I hasten to add that he was not without compliments, though. He once said publicly, in New Shiloh, that one of the things he appreciated about my preaching was that he had never heard me without a sense that I had spent serious time in preparation. Such an observation still blesses my spirit.

I share these father-son interactive ministry moments because one of my father's more prolific gifts was his teaching. As much as I and many throughout Christendom appreciated his prophetic gift, I greatly and tremendously was often mesmerized by his teaching: his teaching of the Bible, his teaching on evangelism, his teaching about theology and most any other associated topic. I've actually witnessed him, for example, giving a Bible lesson based on whatever page that he opened the Bible to and the selected verses he chose to teach from. For some reason, he seemed to think that anyone should be able to do the same. I only needed to be surprised once. After that, I was always "pre-prepared," whether he called on me or not.

Some of us are familiar with the saying, "Not all teaching is preaching, but all preaching, if it's preaching, is teaching." During the years 1994-1997, he co-mentored D.Min. students, with Dr. William Jones, Jr., at United Theological Seminary. To this day, that group of students (preachers and pastors), like

Dr. Claybon Lea, Jr. and Bishop Sir Walter Mack, remark how edified they were to "sit at his feet." One of them, Dr. William Curtis, even took the time to pay tribute to his mentor's teaching and influence in his 2016 Black History Month blog acknowledging among other things, "There are many highly esteemed, educated, and successful trailblazers that deserve to be honored... one of those is the late Rev., Dr. Harold A. Carter, Sr. (who) should be remembered...for the many leaders and ministries that have grown and developed in unbelievable ways with his direction and example." So appreciative were these D. Min. students that they lovingly came to Baltimore from all over the country to serve as pallbearers for my father's Home Going service. Thus, he was effective in the classroom and was able to use that gift and bring the same to his call to preach and wed the two, by the Spirit. He was cerebral, somatic, and anointed. I cannot thank God enough for being able to sit under his preaching ministry and to have his guidance and tutelage. I want to believe that I'm a better preacher because of having done so.

    It is my sense that the Spirit has a way of using those of us who preach in ways that we aren't always aware of. How many times has a preacher preached thinking that the preachment fell on deaf ears, only some time later to have someone share how something that was said had impact on their life? It's no telling how many messages my father may have preached over a period of over 55 years but the likelihood is that the number of those who were impacted that he never heard from will one day be able to share the same with him, on "the other side."

"Honey Upon the Ground," "Love Never Fails," and "The Preaching of Jonah" among other sermons will always resonate in our hearts and minds. I was all the way in Itarsi, India, and seminary students were acting out an original play called "Just Jesus." They told me that they were inspired by my father's message that they had heard with the same title.

I also think that the Spirit uses us in special ways at each stage of our life and does so effectively, regardless of the respective stage or age. I, personally, took some umbrage as my father grew into his seventies when someone, usually another preacher, would say to him, "Dr. Carter, you were vintage," having just heard him preach. The last sermon he preached from the New Shiloh pulpit, as well as regarding his public ministry, in general, was "The Fool Hath Said In His Heart," (Psalm 14:14). His voice was somewhat raspy. His suit jacket was slightly dwarfing his frame due to weight loss, and his steps to and from the pulpit were slow, but his last message was as transformative, powerful and clear as twenty-five years or thirty-five years earlier. In my opinion, my father's preaching was always vintage.

# 8

# The Gospel of Succession

One of the most remarkable aspects associated with the ministry of my father is the way in which God used him throughout his sixty years of preaching and pastoring to influence, mentor, discern, and use men and women as it relates to their respective callings into the Gospel ministry. When God saw fit to release his servant from this side of life's experience, he had been the conduit for more than 130 preachers, having licensed them, as well as having ordained those, as necessary, who met certain requirements. Anyone in "churchdom" will have to admit that such a number is truly an incredible number, making the "womb" of New Shiloh, especially, unique and the leadership of the pastor one of profound nurture and impact. It also speaks to a certain charisma, in my thinking, because we want to connect with those whom we can glean from, be inspired by, and simply feel that they see something in us that we may not see in order that we might aspire to be better.

Without a doubt, association with Pastor Carter, whether direct or indirect, was worn as a badge of honor. His spirit (persona) was a true blessing and made aspiring and veteran preachers and pastors want to spend time with him, probe his mind, and, in many instances, emulate him. His fierce dedication to ministry, his quest to achieve the highest educational degrees, his proven integrity over the years, and his pursuit and love for the craft of preaching, among other character traits, made for the God-breathed blend that we came to know as one of God's great African-American preachers and pastors of the latter 20th century and of the beginning 21st century. Generally speaking, as his "sons" and "daughters," we wanted to be like him and follow him. He was our covering.

The likelihood is that those of us who are used by God to proclaim His Word need covering – spiritual covering. Mavericks of the word or Gospel exist but they're rare. Ideally, and even more importantly, biblically, God's work with regards to the propagation of His Word is usually done via succession. Father, son. Parent, child. Teacher, student. Mentor, mentee. What's more is that, although bloodlines are used and are extremely important, God also has a "spiritual-line."

In practically every discipline, in order for said discipline to continue and thrive, there must be some form of succession. Thomas Hollinger wrote in the *Journal of Biblical Perspectives in Leadership*, "Succession planning and management (SP&M) is a critical process for long-term viability of an organization. Replacement continuity and leadership development are both essential for the process to work effectively."[1]

In spite of his more than full schedule, my father found time, if not made time, to pour himself into the lives of those who found themselves open to his leadership and guidance. Churches, ministries, and preachers/pastors themselves are what and who they are today because they were beneficiaries of the leadership of Dr. Harold Carter. The success of others and their church or ministries can be directly attributed to his success because he made the time to offer advice, spend time with, and dare to avail himself as an example for us to be better prepared to continue to do what he did; albeit, in our own respective ways, given our own respective gifts and talents. From Dr. Charles E. Booth, his first assistant pastor at New Shiloh and present pastor of the Mt. Olivet Baptist Church, Columbus, OH, to Dr. Vincent Thompson, who served as Minister-at-Large before being called to pastor the Community Baptist Church, Newport, RI, to Rev. Doris Gaskins who founded Greater Faith Community Baptist Church, Odenton, MD, and returned to New Shiloh after an effective season of pastoring due to her health, to Rev. Monique T. Carter, Leading Lady of New Shiloh, my wife, and president of the church's Women's Ministry and Ministers Wives Ministry, to Dr. Henry T. Baines, former Minister of Outreach, president of the Ministers and Evangelists Council and Vice-President of the Harold A. Carter Determined Biblical & Theological Institute now living in retirement in Raleigh, NC, to me, his biological and spiritual son, along with all of the other "sons and daughters of the prophet." We owe, in large measure, who we are to who he was in our lives. (Note: during the 1970's, the plethora of licentiates was such that they assumed the biblical nomenclature,

"Sons of the Prophet," which has its biblical roots as having been started by Samuel. In New Shiloh, it soon became known as "Sons and Daughters of the Prophet.")

Samuel, as most know, was the last of the judges, a prophet and a defacto priest. It was Samuel who prepared the way for the transformation of Israel religiously and politically under David. Prior to Samuel, very few people were described as prophets. Arguably, however, Moses was a prophet; an unnamed prophet appears at the beginning of the book of Judges; and Deborah was described as a prophet. Yet, in Samuel's day we read about a group of prophets coming down the hill prophesying (1 Samuel 10:5-13). It is because of this appearance of a group of prophets that tradition asserts that Samuel started a school of prophets. Therefore, although Samuel's sons did not follow him in the role of judge but would be succeeded by Saul and David, in the sense that kings replaced judges, he provided succession in all areas of his ministry.

The Bible gives us other examples of leaders training and preparing their successors. Most familiar is the example of Elijah and Elisha (1 Kings 19:9-21). When Elijah was taken up to heaven, Elisha received a "double portion" of Elijah's spirit becoming his heir and head of the "sons of the prophets" (2 Kings 2).

We also see how Joshua served as an assistant to Moses. Joshua accompanied Moses on Mt. Sinai (Exodus 24:13) and Moses sent Joshua to spy out the land of Canaan with eleven other men (Number 13).

In an ideal world, David would have wanted his own blood, in particular Absalom, to succeed him, but we find that David's own sins caused disruption and that desire did not come to pass. Solomon succeeded him.

Last, we come to Jesus. In Robert Coleman's book, *The Master Plan of Evangelism*, he outlines Jesus' strategy: Jesus called the Apostles first and foremost to be with Him (St. Mark 13:13-14). When they were ready, He gave them jobs and supervised their work (St. John 4:1-2). Then, He sent them out on preaching assignments and debriefed them (St. Luke 9:1-6, 10). Ultimately, He charged them, prior to His ascension with what we call the Great Commission, asking them to make successors themselves in the manner in which they had succeeded Him (St. Matthew 28:18-20). The Apostle Paul continues the work of succession, discipling any number of early church leaders like Timothy and Titus. So, my father, like thousands upon thousands, joined the ranks of those who preceded him as well as those who've succeeded him in the work of spiritual reproduction. Anyone who is established in one's respective work has the burden and responsibility of influence. As such, it should not be taken for granted. When it comes to Kingdom work, it is a privilege to be able to mature to the point whereby one is looked up to for guidance and wisdom.

Beyond being led by God, one of the significant reasons that played a role in my decision to leave the First Baptist Church in Petersburg, VA, and return to the church of my upbringing was the fact that when I accepted my call to preach the Gospel, I was already in college away from home as well as New Shiloh. Unlike most of the "sons" and "daughters" of my father and pastor, I did not have the privilege and really the honor to be with him, to sit under him, as a preacher and subsequently as a pastor. Once I'd accepted my call, doors opened for me for ministry, but those doors kept us apart with regards to the in-person, one-on-one, mentor-mentee relationship. Granted, I'd grown up as the son of a preacher which yielded immeasurable lessons and experiences, but during those formative days, preaching, pastoring and ministry were far from my mind. When the opportunity came for me to *be with* my father "professionally," I couldn't help but want to seize it. He had occasionally conveyed to me that, given the opportunity in life to attach one's self (myself) to God's best, do it. In my estimation, he was one of God's best.

Permit me to briefly share with some specificity, for the sake of background and context, my call and early ministry which ultimately led to my joining my father in pastoral ministry, as well as (and I write this with great reverence) succeeding him.

When I left home to attend Eastern College (now, Eastern University), St. Davids, PA, in the summer of 1979, any notion of returning to live again at home never occurred to me. It wasn't how I was raised, it wasn't an option, and it certainly wasn't an expectation. To the contrary, I had grown up, as most of my friends had, in a culture where it was generally understood that once we, especially as males, graduated high school, we were to find a full-time job, join the military, or go away to college. If one did not go away to college, but attended one locally, one had to find a part-time job and help out with the expenses at home. This really wasn't a big thing. It was simply the way it was.

Actually, I looked forward to going away to college. In the

typical sense of getting out from under everyday parental control, it was somewhat of a liberating experience. My home life was great and greatly appreciated, as I have previously mentioned; however, those omnipresent maternal eyes were especially evident, as even were the paternal.

I entered my freshman year as a Psychology major. I had no real desire to become a psychologist at that particular time. It was that I felt obligated to declare a major and give the impression that I was focused. By the end of my first semester, however, I had been asked by an English professor, Laura Anderson, to tutor students in English grammar. Entering freshmen had to take English 101 as a requirement, and due to my decent high school English skills as acquired at the great and awesome Polytechnic Institute (Go, Poly!), English grammar and writing were proving to open doors for me. I should also add that I had previously tutored preachers at the Virginia Seminary and College Extension in Baltimore while a senior at Poly. Again, my mother taught there and recognized that many of the preachers were lacking basic skills in English. She spoke with the then president, Dr. Eddie Wilson, about her concerns, recommended me, and he gave me a part-time job tutoring several of the men once a week when I'd get out of school.

As I entered my second semester as a freshman, I changed by major to English writing and literature and made Psychology my minor. Ultimately, I would graduate with a double minor in psychology and religion. (Note: Eastern was a liberal arts college, and several foundational courses in religion were mandatory to take. I concluded that since I had to take as many as were required that I would take a few more as were necessary to fulfill the requirements for a minor.) In changing my major, I was beginning to have thoughts of becoming a journalist of some kind. I knew that writing was something I enjoyed, and I knew that etymology and linguistics were interesting to me.

Please know that I was "finding myself" during my freshman year. Again, ministry – preaching and/or pastoring – were nowhere to be found as a consideration. The only reason I was even at a Christian college was because my sister had chosen to go there one year earlier. If I didn't want to pay for college myself, my parents told me that, pending being accepted, Eastern was where I'd be going. My high school grades were decent but they weren't scholarship worthy, not to even mention my math SAT scores.

At some point, I came to some weird resolve in my thinking that I would probably end up being a preacher at some way-in-the-future time. But, believe me, I had no desire to preach, nor did I feel myself being pushed or pulled that way. I can honestly say that my parents never put any such pressure on me at any time. There was, although, a Sunday afternoon dinner conversation which involved Dr. Gardner Taylor, who had preached at New Shiloh that morning. I believe I was about twelve years old and he asked what I wanted to be when I grew up. My response was, "I'd like to be an airplane pilot," at which time both of my parents poo pooed my answer in unison. Then, as a little boy, I'd play church. I'd come home on Sunday afternoons and put on my bathrobe, use my sister's jump rope as a microphone, stand on a foot locker and preach to my sister and her dolls in our playroom. Yes, there were always the voices of family members and others telling me, "You're gonna be like your father when you grow up." Yes, there were moments of biblical astuteness early on in my life. One Saturday, I sat in the back of a preachers' class that my father was teaching. He'd asked them questions about a particular text, which I've since forgotten. What I do remember is that none of them could give the answer he was looking for, and he seemed rather frustrated that they—about twelve of them—couldn't. For whatever reason, he asked me, and I was able to respond correctly. And, yes, I'd given several speeches for youth days and had spoken for Monthly Prayer Breakfasts on several occasions, which went well. Some said that my father was "setting me up" then to see if I had "anything" in me. Notwithstanding, that was the extent of anything resembling any aspiration towards ministry.

All of that would soon change during my first semester as a sophomore while attending college. While returning from a visit with my sister, who was a junior at the time, as I came across the campus, I heard the voice of God say, "Harold, preach!" This unexpected, divine intrusion came without warning or explanation. To say the least, it was startling, yet it was convincing. I could not deny what I had heard.

I can still feel, when I think about it, the deep sense of unworthiness (yes, the "why me?") as I stood on that hill looking out over the campus behind my dormitory, Griffin Hall. A sudden gust of wind blew, shaking the leaves in the trees and forcing tears that had formed as puddles in my eyes to run down my cheeks.

I do not know exactly how long I stood on that hill that

serene Fall evening. Eventually, I went to my room and sat on my bed, trying to discount what had happened. My roommate, Johnny Allen, came in and without hesitation I blurted, "Johnny, I've just been called to preach." In addition to telling my sister the next day, I did not tell anyone else about that night for almost a year.

Shortly after telling my roommate, I walked out into the parking lot. I think I wanted to hear some more or see some cosmic sign affirming that which I already knew and had been affirmed. I stopped walking when I came to the end of the parking lot and stood by a commercial dumpster. It was there when I realized that what I had heard and felt was all I was going to get. Although I did not reveal this experience with anyone other than the aforementioned for some time, I honestly must say that I knew then that the inevitable would come to fruition. I never said, "no," in response. Obviously, I had some soul searching to do, but it was only a matter of time until I would publicly say, "yes."

When I graduated from Eastern College in May of 1983, I'd been licensed and ordained by my father and I'd been called to pastor the Zion Baptist Church, Reading, PA. I'd served as the Youth Pastor at the Saints Memorial Baptist Church, Bryn Mawr, PA, under the pastoral leadership of Dr. Barry Hopkins. One of the members had a sister there who was a member of Zion and recommended me to her to come as a guest preacher on their fifth Sunday Missionary Day. When I arrived that Sunday, after about an hour-long drive, I had no idea that the church was looking for a pastor because the pastor, the late Rev. William Wansley was there. However, after the service, I was asked by the chairman of the deacon board, Dea. Groves, if I had time to meet with the Pulpit Committee. I was stunned but tried not to show it, nor did I ask any questions. My father had told me once, "When God opens a door, don't ignore it. Don't take it for granted. Go through it." His words came to me in that moment. Subsequently, I learned that Rev. Wansley, who was in his senior years, had retired but was still active as a member. During my six years at Zion, he would prove to be a surrogate grandfather and friend, admired not only by me, but also by my father and family, so much so that when Rev. Wansley went home to be with the Lord, my father and my mother came from Baltimore to his homegoing service.

After almost five years at Zion and having attended and graduated from Lancaster Theological Seminary (UCC), Lancaster, PA, where I commuted to three to four days a week, several doors of ministry opened. I had also married my love and God-given wife, Monique, and we had our first son, Daniel, while in Reading. Daniel was born at twenty-six weeks gestation and spent all but the first three months of his existence in neonatology units (NICUs) at the Reading Hospital and the St. Joseph's Hospital for Children, in Philadelphia, PA, respectively. At that time, my weekly take home pay was $475.00. Monique, a cosmetologist, had worked as an operator at a salon in the area and subsequently was blessed to own and operate her own salon, *Nikki's Shear Pleasure* (a name I'd suggested and did the logo for). Her business was doing good, but we both sensed that our days in that area were coming to an end.

Within my fifth year, I'd been called by three churches: The

Union Baptist Church, Hartford, CT; The People's Baptist Church, Baltimore, MD (the pastor, Dr. W. W. Payne, was retiring and recommended me to succeed him. If I had accepted, his further recommendation was that the church would purchase the old New Shiloh edifice on Fremont Avenue and Lanvale Street, which would be vacated once the New Shiloh congregation relocated to its present site, meaning, that at some point I could have been pastoring in the church building I'd grown up in but under a different name.); and the First Baptist Church, Petersburg, VA, said by some, including the renowned African-American historian, Carter G. Woodson, to be the oldest African-American congregation in the United States.[3]

Knowing very little about Petersburg, other than a few Civil War references, I felt that that's where God was leading me along with my family. The Union Baptist Church was strong and stable enough, but we differed on our respective visions regarding evangelism, in general, and what an evangelistic church should be, specifically. With regards to People's Baptist Church, I simply felt that it was not the right time to come back home to Baltimore.

In 1989, we packed up, moved to Petersburg, and I pastored there for seven years. Our second son, Timothy, was born during that pastorate. First Baptist was a challenging but rewarding experience. It was during my fifth year that I received a letter from the New Shiloh Baptist Church, signed by the chairperson, Dea. Elizabeth Adams and the pastor, my father, Dr. Carter. The contents of the letter was to inquire if I might be open to working with my father, Pastor Carter, at some level that would be mutually discussed and defined at a later time, pending my response. Essentially, it was just an exploratory letter of possibility. Since no definitive commitments were being asked, other than my desire, I responded, "Yes." Subsequently, I was informed that, given my openness to the possibility, we, both parties, would pray on it for a year.

Indeed, a full year would pass before I would receive a second correspondence. This time I was asked if I still felt that coming to serve with my father and pastor was a possibility, having prayed about it for a year. Now, keep in mind that I, along with my wife and family, were visiting our families in Baltimore for holidays, etc. I was guest preaching in Baltimore churches, but this process remained confidential and a matter of prayer. So, at the end of the first year, again, my answer was, "Yes." Another full year of prayer would pass.

It was during this time that I'd also received a call from my father. He told me that he'd been diagnosed with prostate cancer and had opted to undergo surgery. I'd never known him to be so transparent as he was during that conversation. Generally, our family tends not to outwardly emote. However, that conversation led to an immediate emotional follow-up call, just to process everything that was and would be going on. Thankfully, the surgery (which I came home to Baltimore for) proved to be generally successful and things soon returned to some normalcy. So, at the end of the second year, I received a third correspondence informing me that, if I was still prayerfully open to the possibility and process, New Shiloh was requesting a face-to-face meeting at my convenience. A date was agreed upon, and I traveled to New Shiloh where I met with my father and pastor, Dea. Adams, and members of the Executive Board of the church. My father moderated the meeting with deference to Dea. Adams.

He explained that three years earlier, Dea. Adams had come to him, saying, "Pastor, with all that you have going on you need some help. Why don't you consider bringing your son here to help you?" He responded, "Dea. Adams, I appreciate what you're saying, but I can't do that. The Lord has to do that." Feeling, however, that two years of praying had given some spiritual impetus, he went on to postulate that if things continued in the direction that those of us at the table believed they would that I would be brought on as "pastor"; that there would not be the usage of the terms "Co-Pastor" or "Senior Pastor," but that the understanding would be (his words) one office—the office of pastor—with two persons. Furthermore, that the congregation would go through the election process and be given the opportunity to vote "yea" or "nay."

After a follow-up meeting with our wives at the table to assure that all parties were on one accord, three years after the first letter and on the strength of several years of prayer, on August 4, 1996, I received a certified letter signed by Dea. Elizabeth Adams indicating that the "New Shiloh congregation voted unanimously to endorse, commend, nominate and elect (me) to the work of pastorate along with (my) father, Dr. Harold A. Carter."

I firmly believe that having been at First Baptist for seven years that the power of God's healing was evident and the congregation was once again growing and moving forward, and although it was a difficult and emotionally charged decision, it was the right time to move on and come "home."

I praise God to this day that my father was led to say what he said and do what he did. Years earlier, my mother had actually suggested the same desire to him, as had Dea. Adams. His choice was to give me the time and space to "establish" myself, develop, start a family, etc. and by abiding by the constitution of the church, as well as for the sake of plain ol' public relations, he was able to circumvent any semblance of nepotism.

My father had to have been acutely aware of the saying that there is no success without a successor. How often has a person's tremendous work, effort, and sacrifice gone with them to the grave? Or, how often has a person's life and legacy been changed and redacted? Effective leaders plan ahead for the time when they can no longer lead. They prepare their successor(s). They model leadership and include their successor(s) strategically, giving them responsibilities and even challenges.

For seventeen years, I experienced the fulfillment of one of my heart's desires: to be with God's best. I listened, observed, tried, and practiced ever appreciating, with each passing year, the incredible gift to the Body of Christ this servant from Selma was. If he were not my father I'm sure I would have been too in awe of him to think that he would ever even take the time to spend with me. God has a way, though. And, I am therefore again grateful to have been his son. How often have we been regretful, or have heard regrets of others, because we did not give flowers to our loved ones while we had the chance or never told them that we loved them. Would I have desired to do and say more? Of course, but I can say, with peace, "no regrets."

He did all he could to remain with us – his family, his church, and his friends. Even in spite of all of the medical confirmations that his time on this earth had essentially come to a close. He had been out of the pulpit for several weeks. I had members of the church share video greetings with him. And, as he lay in the home of my sister, who had become his caregiver, I was able to convince him to record a farewell statement, but he just couldn't seem to rally himself to do it. It wasn't until I suggested that he should pray that he asked for some water, sat up slightly, asked for the curtains to be closed a bit (like he was in a studio), and we began recording. It was an incredible moment and the prayer was transcribed by my brother-in-law, Dr. Henry Davis, and included in the program of his Home Going Service. Just prior to this, his primary physician, Dr. Peter Oroszlan, looked him directly in his eyes and said to him that he wouldn't be going back to New Shiloh. It was then that I thought about recording. I think it was also then that be began to accept the reality of his medical condition. Everything, from a human perspective, that could have been done had been done.

His youngest sister, Blanche (again, familiarly known as Sue) had come from Atlanta, GA, to stay with and help care for him at his home prior to being moved to my sister's home. He had the best of care and medical treatments. He'd been visited by those closest to him, including Dr. John L. Scott, pastor of St. John's Baptist Church, New York, NY, inasmuch as their friendship had become something of a brotherhood, due to the passing of relatives and mutual friends. Countless prayers had gone up on his behalf. He was in the hands of God.

I repeat words that I said during my introductory comments prior to the message I sought to preach for his Home Going Service. As our family sat at our dining room table in our home reminiscing about life, family, church, and current events not knowing that that would be our last Thanksgiving dinner with our beloved father, grandfather, father-in-law, and friend, at some point the after-dinner conversation turned to the subject of height.

Timothy, my (our) youngest son at that time was about 5'11" and still growing. I am 6'1". No one else on the Carter side approaches 6'0". My wife Monique's father was 6'4" and played college basketball. But, again, I'm somewhat unique even going back several generations. The question was raised, I believe by my sister, "Daddy, did it even occur to you that Mann is taller than you?" "Uh, uh," he responded matter-of-factly, and he was dead serious. The conversation briefly went on, only to conclude with him saying that he always thought we were the same height. "Well," as I said from the pulpit where he had stood tall, preaching the Gospel of Jesus Christ in season and out of season, for almost forty-eight years, "Daddy, we weren't the same height. You were and always will be taller than me."

 # Notes

Chapter One: The Gospel of Detroit

1. Harold A. Carter, *A Commemorative Collection: 25th Pastoral Anniversary Journal*, 8.
2. Ibid.
3. Ibid.
4. Ibid., 10.

Chapter Two: The Gospel of Biscuits

1. Jacques Kelly, "Weptanomah Carter, 69, Writer, Founded Youth Center" Obituary, in *The Baltimore Sun*, 2006.
2. Harold A. Carter, *A Commemorative Collection: 25th Pastoral Anniversary Journal*, 13.
3. Jacques Kelly, "Weptanomah Carter, 69, Writer, Founded Youth Center" Obituary, in *The Baltimore Sun*, 2006.
4. Weptanomah W. Carter, *The Black Minister's Wife* (Baltimore: Gateway Press, 1995), 109.

CHAPTER FOUR: THE GOSPEL OF SELF-INSPIRATION
1. Jacques Kelly, "New Shiloh's Rev., Dr. Harold A. Carter, Sr. Remembered at Funeral," in *The Baltimore Sun*, 2013.

CHAPTER FIVE: THE GOSPEL OF ADVENTURE AND A PIONEERING SPIRIT
1. Harold A. Carter, *A Commemorative Collection: 25th Pastoral Anniversary Journal*, 7.
2. Harold A. Carter, *Building Disciples in the Local Church* (Baltimore: Gateway Press, 2005), 12-20.
3. Ibid.

CHAPTER SIX: THE GOSPEL OF DR. QUICK PRAYER
1. Harold A. Carter, *A Commemorative Collection: 25th Pastoral Anniversary Journal*
2. Harold A. Carter, *The Prayer Tradition of Black People* (Valley Forge, PA: Judson Press, 1977).

CHAPTER SEVEN: THE GOSPEL OF THE ENIGMATIC PREACHER
1. Walter S. Thomas, *Dedication of Carter Wax Figure Program Journal*, Great Blacks In Wax Museum, 2014.
2. Larry Williams, *Baltimore Magazine* (November, 1982).

CHAPTER EIGHT: THE GOSPEL OF SUCCESSION
1. Thomas Hollinger, *Journal of Biblical Perspective in Leadership* 5, no. 1, Regent University School of Business and Leadership, 2013.
2. Robert Coleman, *The Master Plan of Evangelism* (Ada, MI: Revell, 2006).
3. Carter G. Woodson, *The History of the Negro Church* (Washington, DC: Associated Publishers, 1921), 62.

 # *Bibliography*

Carter, Harold A. *Building Disciples in the Local Church.* Baltimore: Gateway Press, 2005.

Carter, Harold A. *Determined: A Faith History of A People Determined to Live With Christ!.* Baltimore: Gateway Press, 1984.

Carter, Harold A. *Determined Still.* Baltimore: Gateway Press, 2005.

Carter, Harold A. *The Prayer Tradition of Black People.* Valley Forge, PA: Judson Press, 1977.

Carter, Jr., Harold A. *A Commemorative Collection: 25th Pastoral Anniversary Journal,* 1990.

Carter, Weptanomah W. *The Black Minister's Wife.* Baltimore: Gateway Press: 1995.

Coleman, Robert. *The Master Plan of Evangelism*. Ada, MI: Revell, 2006.

Coppage, Sr., Ernest M. "History of the Black Church" Research Paper. Howard University School of Religion, 2015.

Hollinger, Thomas. *Journal of Biblical Perspective in Leadership 5/1*. Regent University School of Business & Leadership, 2013.

Kelly, Jacques. "New Shiloh's Rev., Dr. Harold A. Carter, Sr. Remembered at Funeral." *The Baltimore Sun*, 2013.

Kelly, Jacques. "Weptanomah Carter, 69, Writer, Founded Youth Center." in Obituary. *The Baltimore Sun*, 2006.

Thomas, Walter. *Dedication of Carter Wax Figure Program Journal*. Great Blacks In Wax Museum, 2014.

Williams, Larry. *Baltimore Magazine*. (November, 1982).

Woodson, Carter G. *The History of the Negro Church*. Washington, DC: Associated Publishers, 1921.

 # *About the Author*

Harold A. Carter Jr.

... is a third generation preacher of the Gospel of Jesus Christ, having been licensed and ordained in the church of his upbringing (1980), the New Shiloh Baptist Church, Baltimore, Maryland.

... is married to Rev. Monique T. Carter, and they are the parents of two sons, Rev. Daniel Carter and Timothy Alphonso Carter. He is the son of the late Dr. and Mrs. (Also Dr.) Harold A. Carter, and has one sister, Weptanomah Davis.

... is a graduate of Eastern College, St. Davids, Pennsylvania, earning a B.A. in English Literature / Writing and Religion.

... is a graduate of the Lancaster Theological Seminary,

Lancaster, Pennsylvania, earning a Master of Divinity degree.

... is a graduate of the United Theological Seminary, Dayton, Ohio, earning the Doctor of Ministry degree, and among many honors and awards, he received the Doctor of Divinity degree from the Virginia Seminary and College, Lynchburg, Virginia, and the Doctor of Humane Letters from Cumberland College, Williamsburg, Kentucky. In 2006, he was inducted into Morehouse College, Atlanta, Georgia, as a Martin Luther King, Jr. Distinguished Preacher.

... is the pastor (since 1996) of the New Shiloh Baptist Church, Baltimore, Maryland, having served along with his father Dr. Harold A. Carter for sixteen years. He leads the congregation of more than 5,000 active members with emphasis on Missions, Evangelism, and Christian Education. His preaching is heard widely throughout this nation, and through radio, television and internet streaming broadcasts. He is credited by his ministerial colleagues and many in the media as galvanizing pastors, activists, community & political leaders, at a time of civil unrest and grief, surrounding the unfortunate death of Freddie Gray, Jr. (allegedly) at the hands of six Baltimore city police officers, to stand in solidarity (with over 200 leaders strong) for a press conference and subsequent March for Peace, which had much to do with quelling the riots and looting and even led to the forging of positive relationships between gang members of the Crips and the Bloods and New Shiloh, along with the faith community.

... formerly pastored the First Baptist Church, Petersburg, Virginia, believed to be the oldest African-American Baptist congregation in America* (1989-1996) and the Zion Baptist Church, Reading, Pennsylvania (1983-1989).

... his ministry has taken him to such places as the Middle East, Romania, Panama, Trinidad, Korea, China, England, the Bahamas, and India, where he has also been privileged to share the Gospel. He sees his **"call"** to the ministry as **"the Divine compulsion to do God's will."**

... has served on a number of boards and conferences. Presently, he serves as the Assistant Secretary of the Hampton University's Ministers Conference and the Executive Secretary for the Global United Fellowship (GUF), which recently (March 2016) afforded him the platform to address the United Nations (UN) in New York, on the subject of "Bridging the Gap Between the Church & Technology." He also presently serves as the President and New Testament / Hermeneutics Professor for the Determined Biblical & Theological Institute of Baltimore, MD. He has served as a Co-Mentor for more than 60 doctoral students at the United Theological Seminary, Dayton, OH. Additionally, he is the Chairperson of the Board of Directors of the New Shiloh Village Development Project a non-profit organization with a goal of community development, including the New Shiloh Senior Living building (an 81-unit facility).

... as an outgrowth of his ministry, publications include:

*The Power of God's Negatives*, *The Sacred Marriage—Getting Started in Pastoral Ministry*, *The Burning Bush*, (co-author), and *Harold's Hermeneutics—Volume One*. Additionally, he has written several songs, three of which have been recorded and performed by New Shiloh's Music Ministry, entitled "You Will Know," "I Never Shall Forget to Praise Your Name," and "Always."

*Woodson, Carter G., *The Story of the Negro Retold*, Associated Publishers, Inc., Washington, DC, 1945, p. 62.

Made in the USA
Charleston, SC
13 July 2016